TALES FROM BROOKGREEN

Also by Lynn Michelsohn

*Roswell, Your Travel Guide
to the UFO Capital of the World!*

by Libby Lynn and Moses James

I See Santa Fe!

TALES FROM BROOKGREEN

Folklore,
Ghost Stories,
and
Gullah Folktales
in the
South Carolina Lowcountry

Lynn Michelsohn

Cleanan Press
Roswell, New Mexico

Tales from Brookgreen
Folklore, Ghost Stories, and Gullah Folktales in the South Carolina Lowcountry
by Lynn Michelsohn

ISBN: 978-0-9771614-5-4
LCCN: 2009925539

First Edition 1.0

Images are used with permission from photographs by:
        Welden Bayliss, pp. 60, 90, 127
        Aaron Michelsohn, pp. 12, 32, 48, 108
        Moses Michelsohn, pp. 80, 87

        Front Cover:
           "The Live Oak Allee at Brookgreen Gardens"
           from a post card by Photo Arts, Inc., Winnsboro, SC

Published by: Cleanan Press, Inc.
        106 North Washington Avenue
        Roswell, NM 88201

Visit our website for more stories and information about Brookgreen Gardens and the Carolina Lowcountry:

www.cleananpress.com

~   ~   ~

For Moses and Aaron,
I hope these recollections convey some of the magic and wonder
of my childhood while engaging your interest in the riches of
your South Carolina heritage.

ACKNOWLEDGEMENTS

The youthful delight that Moses expressed at hearing these stories reminded me of my own enthusiasm for them. Aaron, ever the editor, guided me in writing them down. Alice Duncan typed and retyped. Larry supported this and all my "family stuff." My parents gave me their love and support always. Honey's Horry heritage and Daddy's interest in "local color" shaped my love of the Carolina Lowcountry.

Genevieve Chandler Peterkin encouraged me to recall these stories from my early visits to Brookgreen. She was also kind enough to show me her mother's mysterious Wachesaw beads (after all these years), as well as the Old Methodist Parsonage, and to arrange a family tour of Alice's home in its new location.

The kind hospitality of Mary Emily and Nelson Jackson II repeatedly brought me back to South Carolina. Their daughter Kaki shared her own recollections of our Cousin Corrie's interest in the supernatural with me.

Helen Benso, Vice President of Marketing at Brookgreen Gardens, assisted with this project in several ways including obtaining permission to use materials, correcting factual errors, and providing encouragement.

Most importantly, Cousin Corrie and Miss Genevieve told the tales recorded on these pages. I thank them for sharing their wonderful stories of Brookgreen with all of us who love the Carolina Lowcountry.

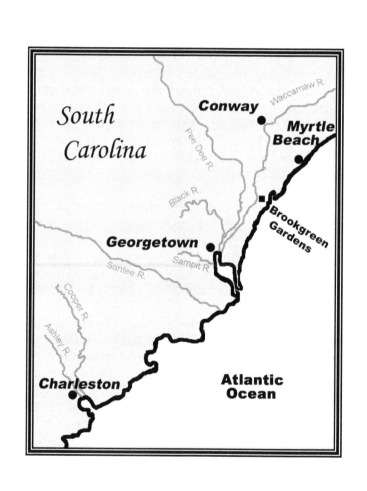

South Carolina

Conway

Myrtle Beach

Brookgreen Gardens

Georgetown

Charleston

Atlantic Ocean

Waccamaw R.

Pee Dee R.

Black R.

Sampit R.

Santee R.

Cooper R.

Ashley R.

Contents

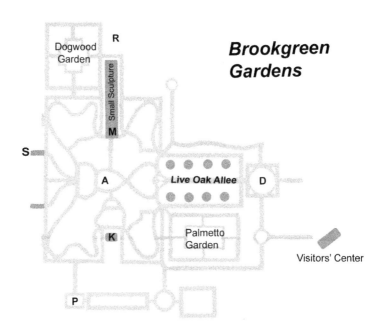

Brookgreen Gardens

Dogwood Garden

R

Small Sculpture

M

S

A

Live Oak Allee

D

K

Palmetto Garden

Visitors' Center

P

KEY

A = *Aligator Bender* Pool
D = *Diana* Pool
K = Old Kitchen
M = Former location of Museum

P = *Pegasus* Pool
R = Former location of Rest Rooms
S = Rice Island Steps

Introduction: The Hostesses of Brookgreen Gardens

One of my greatest treats as a child was to spend the day with Cousin Corrie at Brookgreen Gardens in Murrells Inlet, South Carolina. It was here in the warm Carolina Lowcountry that Archer and Anna Hyatt Huntington had created the first American sculpture garden among the ancient moss-draped live oak trees of four historic rice plantations: Brookgreen, Springfield, Laurel Hill, and The Oaks.

In those simpler days, visitors to Brookgreen Gardens turned off the narrow pavement of Highway 17, the King's Highway, onto two parallel ribbons of concrete spaced far enough apart to support the wheels of a car. Visitors drove slowly along those concrete ribbons through the wooded deer park and past the island of *Youth Taming the Wild* to a sandy parking lot near the *Diana* Pool. There they left their cars in as shady a spot as possible and entered the Gardens on foot, with no admission fee or gatekeeper.

After a leisurely stroll through the Live Oak Allee, with perhaps a detour into the Palmetto Garden, a peek inside the Old Kitchen, and a dip of the fingers into the cool water of the *Alligator Bender* Pool, visitors arrived at the low wide porch of a simple gray-brick building. This structure had once housed the overseer when Brookgreen was a thriving rice plantation. Now it served as the Museum and the entranceway to two open-air galleries for small sculpture. Inside the Museum, steady sounds of splashing water from the *Frog Baby* Fountain in the first gallery created a feeling of sanctuary from summer heat that grew oppressive by mid-morning in the Lowcountry.

This Museum was the Visitors' Center of its day. Here two "sixty-ish" Southern ladies in sturdy shoes welcomed visitors. These two Hostesses were the only staff in evidence throughout the Gardens, other than the occasional groundskeeper trimming ivy. In the cool dim interior of the Museum, Miss Genevieve and Cousin Corrie sold postcards, gave directions, and told stories to visitors interested enough to ask questions about the Gardens.

Boxy glass display cases formed a counter along the front wall of the Museum. Mostly, these cases held stacks of picture postcards. Black-and-white cards sold for five cents, sepia cards for ten cents, and colored cards for twenty-five cents each. Books and pamphlets about the Gardens were also available. Intermixed with this literature stood other items, not for sale, that stimulated frequent questions and often led to Miss Genevieve and Cousin Corrie's stories.

Cousin Corrie, my first cousin one generation removed, was born Cornelia Sarvis Dusenbury in 1888 as her home state of South Carolina emerged from the chaos of Reconstruction. She spent much of her childhood at Murrells Inlet on the Carolina coast and then worked for many years as a schoolteacher and librarian in Florence, South Carolina. In retirement Cousin Corrie returned to Murrells Inlet and joined Genevieve Wilcox Chandler, a writer, artist, and local historian, to become a Hostess at Brookgreen Gardens.

Miss Genevieve was just a bit younger than Cousin Corrie. She had come to Murrells Inlet with her family from Marion, South Carolina but stayed, married, and raised five children here. She often supported them by writing articles on local subjects after the early death of her husband. When the Huntingtons created Brookgreen Gardens they asked Miss Genevieve to become its Hostess.

During my visits to Brookgreen Gardens, Cousin Corrie and Miss Genevieve (as I called her, using the traditional Southern form of address for a grown-up family friend) let me help them with their hostess duties, much to my delight. I also enjoyed playing hide-and-seek among sun-dappled sculptures and looking for painted river turtles sleeping on logs that floated in the old rice field swamps. I loved darting from the shelter of one live oak canopy to the next during summer showers. I especially thrilled at wading in out-of-the-way sculpture pools when no one was looking. But my very favorite activity was listening to Miss Genevieve and Cousin Corrie tell stories of Brookgreen and the Carolina Lowcountry to spellbound Garden visitors, me included.

Each Hostess had her own distinct repertoire. One never encroached on the other's territory. "Now you will have to ask Mrs. Chandler about that," or "Miss Dusenbury can tell you that story," were common responses to visitors' queries. If one or the other of the ladies were absent that day, then the unlucky visitor left without hearing her special tales.

Miss Genevieve tended to cover historical figures and folktales. She had collected local stories for "Mr. Roosevelt" and the 1930s WPA. Cousin Corrie focused on hurricanes, family tales, and accounts of Confederate and Yankee conflicts on the Carolina coast. Her stories related more to her own personal experiences. Of course each had her own unique collection of ghost stories.

I heard some of these stories repeated to countless visitors. The tale of the haunted Wachesaw beads was a frequent favorite. Other stories I only heard once or twice and remember only in snippets, although I have often been able to fill in gaps from other sources. All these stories excited my interest in the historical figures and everyday people who came here before us to the broad rice fields and wooded uplands that became Brookgreen Gardens.

These are the stories Miss Genevieve and Cousin Corrie told, as best I remember them. In my mind these tales weave themselves together with swaying Spanish moss, sparkling splashing fountains, and winding gray-brick latticework of Brookgreen Gardens to create visions of a timeless spirit forever living in the heart of the Carolina Lowcountry.

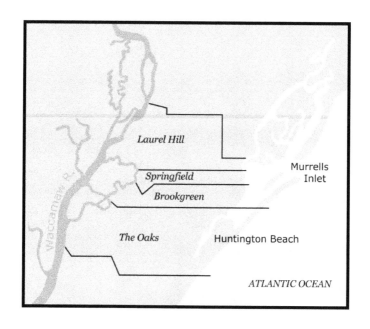

Plantations that became Brookgreen Gardens

The Mistress of Brookgreen

Miss Genevieve always liked to tell visitors about the famous American painter, Washington Allston, called "the American Titian" and "the first great American Romantic painter," who was born at Brookgreen Plantation during the American Revolution. I much preferred her stories about his mother, Rachel, whose long, dramatic, and often romantic life stirred my young imagination.

Rain and wind increased steadily throughout the afternoon and evening along the Carolina coast that fall day in the year 1778. Wealthy Waccamaw Neck rice planter Gentleman Billy Allston and his young wife Rachel had been enjoying their summer on Allston Island but when the weather began to worsen they grew apprehensive. A storm was coming. Horrible September storms sometimes ravaged the Carolina coast. Should they flee inland or brave the gale?

Gentleman Billy and Rachel decided to remain at their summerhouse on the beach that night and luck was with them. The next morning dawned bright and sunny, although debris carried ashore by the still crashing waves told of a shipwreck off the coast. Servants sent to search along the strand found one lone survivor among the disarray of wreckage. As they carried the exhausted man to the nearby Allston beach house, Rachel came out onto the front porch to meet the rescue party. Was the poor man

15

badly injured? She bent over the battered figure gently, then cried out sharply and swooned to the floor! Fearful servants rushed to revive their young mistress, as she was in a delicate condition. Gradually, as she regained her composure, an amazing story emerged.

~ ~ ~

Rachel had been born in the middle of the 1700s on a rice plantation a little north of Charleston, the daughter of John and Elizabeth Vander Horst Moore. They raised her to marry well and within her own social circle, like any other daughter of a wealthy rice planter. She learned to read, write, and understand the simple arithmetic needed to manage a plantation household. She dutifully studied the Church of England's catechism, as well as her obligations to God, King, and family, as she attended services in the small brick church of St. Thomas and St. Denis Parish. Most importantly however, she learned to dance prettily and speak entertainingly of music and the arts as her family spent evenings entertaining other aristocratic rice planter families. Yet Rachel also developed a remarkably independent spirit, unusual for a woman living in those times when a lady was expected to make charming conversation and smile sweetly in submission to the wishes of first her father and then her husband.

In addition to managing his plantation, Rachel's father carried on a successful mercantile business in Charleston and kept a house there. Every year he brought his family to town for the winter social season. It was there that Rachel became engaged to a wealthy and socially prominent young man of Charleston's French Huguenot Neufville family when she was just sixteen years old. Both families blessed the match. However, the wonderful and amazing thing about this engagement, and something that was also unusual for those times, was that these two young people were actually in love with each other! Yet both were still young, and marriage would take place only after Mr. Neufville completed his education in Europe, as was the custom for aristocratic young men of the Lowcountry.

Rachel always enjoyed the social festivities in Charleston but her pleasure in them increased with her engagement. The whirl of parties and balls was exciting for the young couple but the shadow of Mr. Neufville's upcoming departure clouded their happiness. Life was never certain in those times of sudden fevers and stormy seas.

At last the day came when they had to part. Mr. Neufville sailed for Europe and Rachel returned to her family plantation. During the first months of their separation Rachel and her fiancé corresponded regularly in letters filled with promises of undying love. Then his letters ceased. Rachel was at first bewildered and then became anxious. At last came the feared reports of Mr. Neufville's death in a duel in far-off France.

Rachel mourned for many months. Even when new suitors began to present themselves to the charming and wealthy young lady, she could think of little but her lost love. She rejected all who courted her. At first Rachel's family was understanding but then they became impatient and began pressing her to select one of these eligible young men as her husband. Finally, when an extremely wealthy rice planter from that strip of land in South Carolina between the Waccamaw River and the Atlantic Ocean, called the Waccamaw Neck, approached her, she bowed to family pressure and accepted his proposal of marriage. In January 1776, the year of the Declaration of Independence, Rachel married William Allston, a widower with two young children.

Like most rice planters, "Gentleman Billy," as Mr. Allston was often called, owned a house in Charleston where he spent the January and February social season. Most of the year he lived on the Waccamaw Neck as the proprietor of Brookgreen and Springfield Plantations, both of which later became part of Brookgreen Gardens. Each had hundreds of acres of rice lands and hundreds of slaves to tend crops.

Rachel and her new husband made their home at Brookgreen Plantation, named for holdings of the Allston ancestors in England. Heading home after the wedding, the newlyweds took a coastal schooner from Charleston to Georgetown. After crossing Winyah Bay on the ferry to the Waccamaw Neck they elected the land route from there on, their carriage following the narrow King's Highway. About halfway up the Neck they turned off the sandy trail approximately where we do today for Brookgreen Gardens. Soon they entered a lovely avenue bordered by live oaks that Gentleman Billy had created as the final portion of the carriage road leading to his plantation home. Of course, the giant oaks we see today in the Live Oak Allee of Brookgreen Gardens would have been mere saplings in that era.

At the end of the avenue the large but simple plantation mansion built of heart pine and cypress appeared among lush shrubbery, where today the *Alligator Bender* Pool stands. A formal boxwood garden framed the front entrance to the mansion. A broad path behind the mansion led down brick steps to miles of rice islands among the swamps and to the boat dock on a small tidal creek that provided access to the Waccamaw River, the real highway for travel throughout the Lowcountry. Outbuildings circled the barnyard off through the trees in one direction. In the other direction, small cabins for numerous field workers and house servants lined the Street, as that area of slave quarters was called.

Gentleman Billy spent his days at Brookgreen directing the operations of his vast rice empire. He made decisions about financing, planting, harvesting, and selling the crop, as well as handling other administrative matters, while his overseers and drivers directed day-to-day activities on the plantations.

Rachel's marriage had brought her a large household to manage. She took over these duties with enthusiasm, supervising preparation of food for storage as well as day-to-day preparation of meals, work that took place in the separate kitchen building still standing today at Brookgreen Gardens. She also supervised, and sometimes assisted with, making clothing for the workers from cloth spun and woven on the plantation, and making garments for her own family from finer material purchased from Charleston importers. Nursing, gardening, child rearing, and early education were also usual duties of the plantation mistress. Of course, when friends, relatives, or dignitaries occasionally visited, Rachel made a lively and charming hostess. During the first years of her marriage she developed into one of the most gracious hostesses on the Waccamaw Neck.

Sundays were devoted to religious activities. The family, accompanied by favored servants, often attended morning worship at the official Church of England All Saints Parish Church, just a few miles south of Brookgreen Plantation. They spent the remainder of the day in rest, religious study, or other quiet activities suitable to the Sabbath.

Rachel and Gentleman Billy were happy together, although their relationship was described as more respectful than passionate. Rachel mothered William's young children as her own. One wonders however, how often her thoughts might have strayed to Mr. Neufville, her first love.

Each year the Allston family spent the midwinter social season at their house in Charleston. There Rachel had the opportunity to renew her friendships, visit with relatives, and rejoin the social whirl. Gentleman Billy devoted a great deal of his time to both political discussion and horse racing activities. The Allston family still owns a silver bowl, beautifully engraved by Paul Revere, won by one of Gentleman Billy's racehorses during the Charleston race meets.

Each February at the close of the Charleston social season, Rachel and Gentleman Billy returned to Brookgreen Plantation. They remained here until warming weather signaled the need to leave the rice lands for a healthier location. Some planter families maintained homes in the cool mountains but Gentleman Billy built a summerhouse high in the dunes toward the northern end of their own barrier island just across the King's Highway from the main body of Brookgreen Plantation. This area was known then as Allston Island and later called Theaville, then Magnolia Beach. Today it is known as Huntington Beach.

Each year in late spring Rachel would supervise the move of her household from the plantation mansion to the summerhouse, only a few miles away. Servants packed clothing, mattresses, bedding, sewing materials, and medicines from the upstairs; cooking utensils, pots, pans, and washing equipment from the kitchen; china, glassware, linens, and silverware from the dining room; food, wine, and liquors from the cellars; books, papers, pens, and inks from the library; musical instruments, toys, and games from the drawing room; and hunting and fishing gear from the storage room. They transported everything they needed for several months by wagon to the seashore.

At the beach, life continued on as usual in the Allston household throughout the summer and early fall, although the manner was slightly less formal. The close distance allowed them easy access to the main part of the plantation. Gentleman Billy was able to ride over to the rice fields during the day to check on the progress of the crops and to attend to other business when necessary. He could still return to the beach to escape the deadly "mal-arias" that arose from the swamps every evening.

Fresh fish, crabs, and shrimp were readily available on Allston Island. Fresh vegetables arrived regularly from plantation gardens. Sea breezes were wonderfully cooling, and while sea bathing was not yet in vogue, long strolls along the strand provided delightful entertainment, as did watching the never ceasing waves and the soaring diving shore birds. It was only in the fall that sea breezes turned into worrisome gales that sometimes devastated the coast.

And this September, there on Allston Island, one of these storms had brought Rachel something unimaginable! Mr. Neufville lay at her feet. Was this a ghost? Or had her long lost fiancé returned from the dead? Mr. Neufville had certainly come back to Rachel, but too late. She was now the Mistress of William Allston's Brookgreen Plantation, and she was expecting his child.

History does not tell us anything further about the reunion of the two former sweethearts or about what happened to Mr. Neufville after his recovery. Presumably he returned to his life in Charleston. Perhaps he married another planter's daughter. After his dramatic return to the Lowcountry he passed out of our story. Rachel's adventures continued, however.

~   ~   ~

Rachel and Gentleman Billy remained happily at Brookgreen Plantation and soon celebrated the birth of their daughter, Mary. As the American Revolution gained momentum in the South they supported the Revolutionary cause with great conviction. Gentleman Billy contributed money for the relief of Boston following the Tea Party and loaned money to the state of South Carolina for its war effort. His Brookgreen Plantation served as a transfer point for gunpowder that local Patriots shipped from Georgetown to Rebel forces in Wilmington, North Carolina. When their next child was born in 1779, Rachel and Gentleman

21

Billy named him Washington Allston, in honor of the Commander-in-Chief of the American forces.

But the War was not going well for the Americans. When Charleston fell to the British, the spirits of South Carolina Patriots fell as well. Georgetown was the most important city in South Carolina still in Patriot hands and the British soon threatened it. Gentleman Billy sent workers from Brookgreen Plantation to help with fortifications at Georgetown but Lord Cornwallis' superior forces soon captured that city too. Prospects for American Patriots looked grim.

Fortunately, new hope soon began to stir as Rebels in South Carolina shifted their fighting tactics. Although they could no longer confront the superior British forces on the formal field of battle, General Francis Marion, who had barely escaped capture at the fall of Charleston, organized bands of guerilla fighters to harass the British along the South Carolina coast. Marion's men would strike unexpectedly, then disappear into Lowcountry swamps, earning him the nickname of "The Swamp Fox" from frustrated British generals.

Many local Patriots, including our Miss Dusenbury's relatives, joined his guerilla bands. Gentleman Billy, who happened to be General Marion's brother-in-law, soon became a Captain in the Swamp Fox's command and led several successful raids on British troops in our area.

Although Gentleman Billy was often able to return home to Brookgreen Plantation between raids, Rachel was forced to take on more day-to-day management of both Brookgreen and Springfield Plantations. Her spirit and her intelligence enabled her to keep the vast plantations operating successfully in spite of military and economic disruptions of the period.

Once Lord Cornwallis became commander of British forces in the South and captured both Charleston and Georgetown, he contemplated his next step toward victory in the American colonies. His plan was to march his troops northward to Virginia to crush George Washington's poorly prepared forces gathering there. Much to Lord Cornwallis' annoyance however, General Marion's guerrilla attacks forced him to keep his troops in South Carolina attempting to control the countryside. Frequent skirmishes and several larger battles continually delayed his plans. It took another year before Lord Cornwallis could finally advance his troops northward to Yorktown to meet General Washington's army, an army that was ready for the British by that time. And we all know how that turned out.

During the time Lord Cornwallis remained in South Carolina, fighting was fierce, even if it only occurred in brief spurts. Not only were American soldiers fighting British soldiers but more often, South Carolina Patriots were fighting South Carolina Tories who were usually neighbors and often even relatives. Atrocities occurred on both sides but one of Lord Cornwallis' officers, Colonel Banastre Tarleton, became infamous for particularly nasty treatment of captured troops and of Patriot supporters and their families.

Thus it was with horror that Rachel received news one morning while Gentleman Billy was away with the American forces that Lord Cornwallis had selected Brookgreen Plantation as his temporary headquarters. Everyone knew that "Bloody Banastre" had recently slaughtered American soldiers who surrendered to him and had burned the family home of another South Carolina Patriot, General Thomas Sumter, "The Fighting Gamecock." Rachel feared what Lord Cornwallis' troops might do to her plantation. Even more, she feared what they might do to herself and to her children, the family of one of General Marion's well-known officers.

In spite of her fears, Rachel bravely and graciously welcomed Lord Cornwallis and his staff as they rode up the Live Oak Allee to take up residence in her home. To her surprise and relief, Lord Cornwallis and his officers conducted themselves with equal courtesy. They behaved more like gentlemen staying in the home of a friend than enemies occupying a requisitioned household. All were extremely kind and courteous to Rachel and encouraged her to continue running the household and plantation without disruption.

While playing gracious hostess to her unwelcome visitors, Rachel made every effort to keep her children out of sight of Lord Cornwallis and his staff. This was especially true for her young son, Washington, named for the commander of the American forces. In spite of her best efforts however, the British learned of this Washington's existence from servants.

One day at dinner, to Rachel's sudden terror, Lord Cornwallis announced that he had heard that a young Washington resided in the household and commanded his hostess to present her son to the company. Inwardly trembling with fear, she could not help but comply with his demand. With outward calm she sent for the toddler. When he arrived Rachel formally introduced Washington to Lord Cornwallis and then carried him around the dining room, presenting him to each officer. To her surprise and delight, Lord Cornwallis and his officers "oohed" and "aahed" over the boy, playfully tweaking the cheeks of "The Little General."

Later, Lord Cornwallis and his troops moved on northward leaving Brookgreen Plantation entirely intact. Nothing was stolen or damaged. Perhaps this was because of their respect for Rachel Moore Allston, the spirited but gracious young Mistress of Brookgreen Plantation. Rachel had once again weathered a challenging encounter . . . and her story continued.

~   ~   ~

As the war wore on, Gentleman Billy and his troops moved north, joining the larger body of General Nathaniel Greene's Continental Army. The despair of the American forces in the South that had come with the British occupation of Charleston and Georgetown gradually turned to joy with decisive American victories at the Battles of Kings Mountain and Cowpens along the border of North and South Carolina.

Gentleman Billy, now Captain Allston, fought bravely and successfully in the Battle of Cowpens but difficult living conditions in the swamps and on the march had taken their toll. As the battle ended, fever wracked his body. Gentleman Billy bid farewell to his men and started the long ride back to his home on the Waccamaw Neck. After several days his horse at last turned off the King's Highway into the familiar oak-lined avenue of his Brookgreen Plantation. As Rachel and the house servants rushed out to meet him, Gentleman Billy dismounted and then collapsed onto the front steps of his plantation mansion, too weak to stand. Servants carried him inside to his bed where he died in Rachel's arms before nightfall.

~   ~   ~

Once again grief filled Rachel's heart. But now she was alone with five children: Billy's son and daughter from his first marriage and her own three young children, including a newborn son. Nevertheless, Rachel took over management of Brookgreen and Springfield Plantations, this time on her own. Although family members helped when they could, primary responsibility for plantation operations fell on her.

Months passed. Lord Cornwallis surrendered at Yorktown and America had won its independence. Soldiers began returning to their homes and families. The disrupted life and economy of South Carolina started to return to normal.

One day an unknown gentleman unexpectedly rode up the Live Oak Allee of Brookgreen Plantation and presented himself at the plantation mansion, asking for Captain Allston. He introduced himself as Dr. Henry Collins Flagg, most recently, head surgeon with General Nathaniel Greene's Continental Army. Dr. Flagg explained that he was originally from Rhode Island but had come south to seek his fortune before the war. When Americans began raising troops, he had joined General Greene's army as a surgeon and had met Captain Allston during General Greene's Southern Campaigns. Captain Allston had described the beauty of his Waccamaw homeland and had invited Dr. Flagg to visit him at Brookgreen Plantation after the war.

Rachel welcomed Dr. Flagg graciously, as ever, but informed him sadly of the death of her husband. Dr. Flagg was grieved to hear of the loss of his friend and did everything he could to comfort and assist the widow, extending his stay to help Rachel manage day-to-day affairs of the plantations. He took special interest in the Allston children, and they readily enjoyed the interest and kindness of their new friend. As weeks and months passed, Rachel and Henry fell in love and talked of marriage.

Rachel was happy at last after so much heartache and strife but an obstacle to this happiness quickly arose. Rachel's family in Charleston adamantly opposed her marriage to Dr. Flagg. They called him a "Yankee adventurer" who was only interested in her fortune. Rachel's father threatened to disinherit her if she proceeded with the marriage. But Rachel, true to her nature, determined to marry him anyway! She told friends, "I married to please my family the first time but this time I will marry to please myself." And she did.

~   ~   ~

Rachel and Henry Flagg settled down to married life on Brookgreen Plantation. The marriage was a long and loving one. Dr. Flagg took a fatherly interest in his step-children and was especially close to young Washington Allston, who became one of the first world-renowned American painters (but that's another story).

Rachel and Henry Flagg had three additional children together. Their grandchildren included Dr. Allard Belin Flagg, who lived in the Hermitage, and his sister Alice, who still may (another story). They also included Dr. Allard's brother, Dr. Arthur Belin Flagg, who, along with most of his family, suffered terribly in The Flagg Flood of 1893 (but that is yet another story).

It was from their home at Brookgreen Plantation that Dr. Flagg set out on a special mission one fine June afternoon in the year 1791. Exciting news had traveled down the Waccamaw Neck: President George Washington was passing through this area on his tour of the southern states. Dr. Flagg hoped for a chance to meet him, or at least for a chance to see the hero of the Revolution and the "Father of our Country."

Early in his presidency George Washington had vowed to tour the entire country, seeing the land, gauging the prosperity, and getting to know the thoughts of the people. (Remember, there were only thirteen states to visit back then!) He had already made a New England Tour in 1889 and had begun planning his Southern Tour as soon as he returned home, which was in Philadelphia at that time. (The official capital of the United States was there until they built a capital city from scratch in the District of Columbia.)

President Washington planned his route carefully, intending to visit cities along the coast as he headed south and then to include more inland cities on his return north. He determined just how long each part of the journey would take and corresponded with officials in every city along the route, letting each know exactly when he planned to arrive. Officials thus had time to plan welcoming celebrations, some of which were amazingly elaborate.

As soon as Congress adjourned in March 1791 President Washington began his Southern Tour. He left Philadelphia on March 21st preferring to face bad weather in the early weeks of the trip rather than be caught during the summer "sickly season" in the South when many died of malaria and yellow fever.

President Washington's plan was to stay at inns and hotels so that he would not inconvenience, or become beholden to, private citizens, although he had numerous offers of lodging from wealthy supporters. This plan had worked well during his New England Tour but in the sparsely populated South the only lodging he could find was often in a private home. That was certainly the case along the many desolate miles of the sandy King's Highway here on the Waccamaw Neck.

As Dr. Flagg rode north along the King's Highway that day he first heard clatter, then saw an amazing sight coming around a bend. Four beautifully matched white horses emerged from behind the trees. Red leather harnesses with golden hardware linked them to a white coach driven by an imposing man in red and white livery. Beside him perched a footman in a similar outfit.

The coachman reined the team to a stop as he saw Dr. Flagg. Dr. Flagg also stopped, gazing in wonder at the splendid carriage, as well he should. George Washington had ordered one of his own coaches refurbished magnificently for the tour. Paintings of the four seasons adorned the side doors, front, and back of the carriage. The Washington coat of arms gleamed within ovals on the quarter panels and glass windows shaded by Venetian blinds faced forward. The framework, springs, moldings, and door handles were all golden, not an every-day sight even among wealthy rice planters of the Waccamaw Neck.

After they exchanged greetings President Washington explained to Dr. Flagg that he and his party had entered South Carolina from North Carolina the day before and had spent the night at Jeremiah Vareen's Boundary House. That morning they had crossed Singleton Swash (near today's Windy Hill Beach) at low tide and rolled along the hard-packed sand of what is now Myrtle Beach for sixteen miles. Five miles along (about where Myrtle Beach State Park is located today) they had eaten their midday meal with rice planter George Pauley III, who had fought in the Revolution. From there they had continued on south along the beach, then followed the King's Highway through thick forest when it turned inland to avoid marshes. Now they were unsure as to where they would spend their next night.

Dr. Flagg graciously invited the President and his entourage to stay at Brookgreen. They accepted gratefully and followed Dr. Flagg on down the sandy trail to Brookgreen Plantation. The fabulous coach, which President Washington called his "chariot," was soon rolling through the Live Oak Allee up to the plantation mansion. A baggage wagon with additional servants and several saddle horses followed behind. There, by today's *Alligator Bender* Pool, President Washington alighted to be greeted by Rachel Moore Allston Flagg, the Mistress of Brookgreen, and her children including "The Little General," Washington Allston.

It was in this way that President Washington spent his first night on the Waccamaw Neck at Brookgreen Plantation before heading on south to glorious celebrations at

Clifford Plantation on the lower Waccamaw Neck, then to Georgetown, Charleston, and Savannah. No doubt, as she entertained the President at dinner, Rachel Flagg told him the story of Lord Cornwallis' introduction to young Washington Allston.

~ ~ ~

Gentleman Billy Allston had left Brookgreen Plantation to his eldest son, Benjamin (from his first marriage), and Springfield Plantation to his second son, Washington. Rachel and Henry Flagg continued to live at Brookgreen until the boys were old enough to manage the plantations themselves.

Benjamin and Washington Allston reached adulthood and took over their plantations around the turn of the century. Each quickly disposed of his inheritance (again, another story; there are so many tales connected to Brookgreen Gardens). At that time Rachel and Henry Flagg left Brookgreen Plantation for the home near Charleston that Rachel's father had willed to her, in spite of his threats of disinheritance. There, Rachel and Henry lived out their days enjoying each other's company and that of their children and grandchildren. They were buried next to each other at Rachel's childhood St. Thomas and St. Denis Parish Church, forever together.

And so ends the story of the plucky Mistress of Brookgreen Plantation and the man she finally married for love: a romantic ending to a long and dramatic story, and to a long and dramatic life.

The Mistress of Brookgreen

Don't T'ief!

Cousin Corrie occasionally recounted stories that old "Dr. Wardie," beloved physician of Brookgreen Plantation (and a great-grandson of Rachel and Henry Flagg) had told her many years previously. This was a story Dr. Wardie had heard from his aunt, "Miss Bessie." He, Cousin Corrie, and Miss Bessie all enjoyed the story because it revealed that high and mighty rice planters of olden times didn't always have everything their own way.

Although the rice harvest was bountiful that year in the mid-1800s on Brookgreen Plantation the plantation Overseer was troubled. The yield in rice didn't seem to be as large as he had expected. The Overseer thought and thought about this and finally became convinced that someone was stealing rice from the barn where they stored it after threshing.

But who could be taking the rice, and how? No one could steal rice during the day with so many people about, yet how could anyone get into the rice barn at night? It was locked carefully each evening and there were no signs of break-in.

Suddenly the Overseer realized who locked the barn each evening! Devine, the head slave on the plantation, held the keys. Old stories began to recall themselves to the

Overseer, stories about Devine stealing rice and selling it to buy liquor (and of how Devine had gotten caught but I won't go into that right now).

"So!" mused the Overseer to himself, "Devine is sneaking into the barn at night and stealing rice again! And he is probably bringing other slaves with him because a lot of rice seemed to be missing. Now how can I catch Devine and his accomplices in their act of thievery?"

The Overseer thought, and thought some more, and finally devised a plan. He would hide in the rice barn at night and surprise Devine when he and the others came in to steal rice. And he would put his plan into effect that very evening!

After the day's work was completed the workers all went home to the Street, as the community of slave cabins was called. The Overseer also went home to his cottage near the Street but after dark he crept back to the rice barn, which was located where the Dogwood Garden stands today at Brookgreen Gardens, just behind us here in the Museum. The Overseer looked around stealthily but all was still. He unlocked the door, slipped into the barn, and carefully relocked the door from the inside.

The rice barn was not a very inviting place to spend the night but the Overseer made himself a pallet out of rice straw and curled up near the door to wait. He didn't bother to stay awake because he knew that anyone entering the barn would rouse him.

The next morning the Overseer awoke nicely rested. His sleep had not been disturbed by anyone coming into the barn. Disappointed but undaunted, he slept in the barn again the next night, with the same results.

This puzzled the Overseer greatly. Why wasn't his plan working? He thought some more and decided that

Devine must have known somehow that he was sleeping in the rice barn. Of course Devine and the others would avoid coming in to steal rice with him there. So that evening the Overseer made a big show of moving his pallet out of the barn and giving up his attempt to catch anyone coming into the barn at night. But as soon as it was dark he sneaked out of his cottage and crept back to the rice barn. This time he hid himself in the trees along the edge of the barnyard where he could keep close watch on the barn without being seen.

The Overseer sat for hours watching in the dark, again with no results. No moon or stars shone through the cloudy skies and night noises made him uneasy at times but he was determined to catch his thief.

Suddenly a faint light appeared at the far edge of the barnyard. The Overseer's initial thrill quickly turned to apprehension. This was a very strange looking light. It was not a torch but a faint, eerie glow. Gradually his apprehension turned to terror. All the stories he had ever heard about haunts and plat-eyes came rushing back to him as the faint glow bobbed slowly along the far tree line. What manner of horrifying specter was coming from the miasmic swamps to threaten him? At least it wasn't coming any closer!

Slowly the glow moved toward one of the outbuildings in the barnyard, the one where workers stored rice straw after they threshed the rice grains out of it. Nothing was wasted on the plantation and even worthless rice straw made good animal bedding or compost for cornfields.

In another moment a light flared inside the outbuilding as if someone had lit a torch. Suddenly the explanation came to the shaken Overseer: the faint glow that he had watched bob along the tree line had come from a glowing ember carried hidden in a pot. Now someone had used that ember to light a torch inside the building.

Fear drained from the Overseer to be replaced by curiosity. What was anyone doing sneaking into the shed where they stored rice straw? The Overseer moved closer until he could see inside the building. A large muscular slave stood with his back to the doorway holding a small "fat light'erd," a splinter of pine heartwood saturated with pine resin that served as a torch, illuminating the inside of the building. Under his direction three field hands dug down into the piles of straw and pulled out seagrass baskets. From the baskets they poured rice into sacks.

When the sacks were full and tied closed the workers hoisted them over their shoulders. The man with the torch then turned to lead them out and the Overseer could see him clearly. It was not Devine. It was John! One of Captain Ward's most trusted field hands, and the plantation Class Leader!

As the Overseer watched, John extinguished his torch. He and the others stole back out into the night and headed toward their homes in the Street. The Overseer understood that later they would pound the rice in homemade mortars hidden in the swamps to remove the outer hulls, then boil it up for dinner in their cabins in the Street. Not only would they have extra rice to stretch their weekly rations, but fancy whole-grain rice even better than the midlins, which are the broken grains that could not be sold on the international market, that Captain Ward and his family ate, and certainly better than the small broken pieces the slaves usually got in their weekly food ration.

Now the whole situation became clear. No wonder he hadn't caught his rice thief by sleeping in the barn. Devine was not stealing rice from the barn. Nobody was stealing rice from the barn! And Devine was not involved at all. The thief was John!

Each day as field workers threshed the rice and scooped it into baskets, they hid some of the baskets in bundles of straw instead of taking them to the rice barn. Then when they carried the bundles of rice straw into the outbuilding for storage they were also carrying away hidden baskets of the newly threshed grain. Later they easily returned during the night to collect the hidden rice from under the straw in the unlocked shed. There was no need to steal rice from the carefully locked rice barn!

The Overseer had discovered his thieves at last. And the biggest shock was that John, the plantation Class Leader, was leading them in their thievery!

Class Leaders, Parson Belin, and the Methodist Mission to the Slaves

Now I should tell you something about what it meant to be a Class Leader and why it was so shocking that a Class Leader would be involved in stealing.

For you to really understand about Class Leaders I have to explain about the Methodist Mission to the Slaves on the Waccamaw Neck. That all started with Parson James Lynch Belin (which he pronounced "Blane"), who was a great-uncle of Dr. Wardie, the man who told me this story.

James Belin grew up in Charleston in a wealthy planter family. Like all planters' sons he was educated for life as a planter himself. His older brother, Allard Belin, enjoyed the politics and mercantile dealing that made up a planter's life but James did not, although he accepted the vocation that his family had planned for him.

When James reached adulthood in the early 1800s, his father gave him the management, and later the ownership, of Wachesaw Plantation here on the Waccamaw Neck (we don't know the exact details, thanks to General Sherman, but that's another story). James was quite content to move to the Waccamaw Neck. He had always preferred the quiet isolated lifestyle of planters here to the social whirl and political intrigues in Georgetown and Charleston that so engaged his older brother.

Additionally, James' favorite sister, Margaret, and her husband, Dr. Ebenezer Flagg, made their home here. Dr. Eben, as he was known, was the son of Dr. Henry Flagg and Rachel Moore Allston Flagg of Brookgreen Plantation (remember them?). Dr. Eben had not inherited any land on the Waccamaw Neck but he contracted his medical services to other planters to take care of their families and their large populations of slaves.

Because of their close proximity and compatibility, James grew especially attached to Eben and Margaret and to their growing family. He never had children and soon came to view the Flagg children almost as his own. He shared Eben and Margaret's joy at the birth of each child and then their sorrow at the early death of their first-born son, Allard Belin Flagg, named in honor of Margaret and James' successful brother Allard (perhaps in the hope that wealthy Brother Allard would become a patron to his namesake, as was often the custom at that time).

When Eben and Margaret had another son, James encouraged them to name him Allard Belin Flagg II, in remembrance of their beloved firstborn as well as their successful brother. James enjoyed the other Flagg children, including Arthur and Alice, but always took a special interest in Allard and even gave him Wachesaw Plantation when he became an adult.

Of course, like most planters, James Belin had been raised in the Episcopal Church. Like many in the Carolina Lowcountry in the early 1800s however, he was curious about early Methodist bishops who traveled these wild areas by horseback, holding camp meetings and revivals where they expounded fiery new doctrines that challenged established teachings of the Episcopal Church. He heard both Bishop Asbury and Bishop Coke preach in their travels through the Lowcountry. James soon "caught the spark of this new fire." He traveled to hear Methodist preaching as often as he could and decided to dedicate his life to spreading the Word of God as Methodists understood it to be. Bishop Asbury himself ordained James Belin as a Methodist minister.

Now Methodism had run into one major stumbling block in South Carolina. Basic tenets of Methodism held that slavery was wrong. You can imagine that this teaching did not sit too well with the powers-that-be, most of whom were large slave owners. It was bad enough having to deal with Northern abolitionists but now to have charismatic preachers traveling throughout the countryside teaching that God's Word spoke against the very institution that formed the basis for their whole way of life was just too much! Wealthy and powerful planters began to oppose this new religion with vigor.

Methodist bishops soon recognized that practical considerations demanded a change in Church policy. Using logic along the lines of "Render unto Caesar what is Caesar's," the Methodist Church decided that in areas where the law sanctioned slavery, they would not press this issue.

Perhaps as a way to soothe their consciences, Church leaders established a Methodist Mission to the Slaves that rapidly gained support in the Carolina Lowcountry as well as in other Southern states.

This Mission gave slaves in the American South the same chance to receive the benefits of God's Word and the teachings of Christ that Methodist Missions to Africa and China gave other non-Christians.

Before the early 1800s, nobody had paid much attention to the religion of slaves who worked the plantations. Most slaves had brought their tribal religions with them from Africa, of course, and still practiced them as far as possible in their new circumstances. Planters suppressed practices that they considered blatantly heathen but most African practices and beliefs remained strong, if hidden, and many still do today. The whole subject of Hoodoo and conjure doctors and protective spells and evil spirits is one that outside people know very little about.

Many slaves readily accepted the new Christian religion when it was offered to them. That is not to say that they necessarily gave up their old religions but this new one seemed a good addition to deal with their concerns in America, and it did offer hope of a better life to come in the Promised Land, a land where all toils and tasks were over.

So James Belin became a Methodist preacher and he found all the work he would ever need right around him. He continued to operate his Wachesaw Plantation but devoted himself to the Methodist Church's Mission to the Slaves on the Waccamaw Neck.

At first Parson Belin's neighbors were shocked by the idea of his mission. At times they actively discouraged his efforts so he started out preaching only to his own slaves on Wachesaw Plantation. He was soon able to convince Robert and Francis Withers, who by that time owned nearby Brookgreen and Springfield Plantations, to let him minister to their slaves as well.

On Sundays, always a day of rest on plantations, Parson Belin preached the Gospel to slaves gathered outdoors under the shade of spreading live oak boughs. He held catechism classes for adults and children where he taught them to recite the questions and answers of Methodist doctrine from memory. But more was needed. In those days, joining the Methodist Church was not a simple matter. The Methodist Church required serious study and a period of probation for prospective members before baptism and being admitted to "the Communion of Saints, the Forgiveness of Sins, the Resurrection of the Body, and the Life Everlasting." Parson Belin could not do all the teaching himself so he selected a slave from each plantation who could read and write at least a little to become the Class Leader. Under Parson Belin's instruction, Class Leaders read and studied the Bible and other religious tracts, then taught their fellow slaves what they had learned. In this way Class Leaders prepared their class members to be baptized and to join the Methodist Church.

Becoming a Class Leader was quite an honor. It was also a way to gain special privileges among plantation slaves. Only the most intelligent, educated, diligent, and outwardly moral were selected for this great honor and position of trust. Each worked hard to maintain himself as a model of pious devotion to the tenets of Christianity. And each led the constant effort to seek out and severely chastise anyone in the slave community whose behavior might be unacceptable in the eyes of God, or the plantation master. The Class Leader became the paragon, as well as the enforcer, of moral righteousness on each plantation.

Parson Belin made a good start in the early years of his Mission to the Slaves, but then the Vesey Rebellion, a thwarted slave uprising in Charleston in 1822, brought the Mission to the Slaves to a standstill.

Planters throughout the Lowcountry began to oppose the Mission because they believed that instruction and organization by slave Class Leaders had encouraged the Vesey Rebellion. Hysteria of all sorts took hold. In spite of this Parson Belin continued his work.

Finally, after the furor had died down, more planters began to recognize the benefits of the Mission to the Slaves. In addition to any concerns they might have had for their slaves' spiritual welfare, planters began to see practical advantages in teaching them the Christian Gospel. In the planters' eyes these teachings promoted stability on the plantation by encouraging order, obedience, and morality among slaves and by reducing lawlessness and the most obvious vices.

In fact, in addition to supporting Parson Belin's work, Waccamaw Neck planters began encouraging their own Episcopal Church to bring Christian teachings to their slaves. Reverend Alexander Glennie of All Saints Episcopal Church later became well known for his missionary work among slaves and for the numerous slave chapels he convinced planters to build on the Waccamaw Neck. But it should not be forgotten that in the early years, it was Parson Belin who started this whole movement in our area. For many years it was only he who brought the Christian Gospel to the slaves. He was the one who taught them hymns of the Methodist Church that they developed into their rich body of Gullah spirituals. He was the one who selected and developed Class Leaders, and even slave preachers, who became spiritual and political leaders of their people in the turbulent years that followed.

When Colonel Joshua John Ward bought Brookgreen Plantation from the Withers family in the 1830s he encouraged Parson Belin and his assistants to continue working among his slaves.

So did Colonel Ward's son, Captain Joshua Ward, after he inherited Brookgreen and Springfield Plantations in the 1850s. (Of course Joshua Ward wasn't a Captain then; that came later when he took command of the Wachesaw Riflemen and then the Waccamaw Light Artillery during the War but I still think of him as Captain Ward and I'll call him that.)

Old Colonel Ward (and I don't know why he was called Colonel) had been a stern but fair master, respected by his slaves and the white community alike. Young Captain Joshua Ward continued this tradition. He and his wife Bessie were generally liked and respected by their workers. The plantations ran smoothly under his management and Class Leaders on them continued to be highly respected men among their fellow slaves and among planters.

Captain Ward had grown to admire John, the Class Leader on his Brookgreen Plantation. John was a tall strong man, a good worker, and a leader among his people. As a field hand he became expert in all phases of rice production. Captain Ward came to rely on John more and more because of his intelligence, his expertise, his leadership abilities, and especially because of his honesty. The plantation Overseer was not quite so trusting of John and sometimes resented Captain Ward's reliance on John's judgment in matters related to the rice growing operation. But Captain Ward continued to entrust John with numerous responsibilities and to praise his abilities and loyalty.

The year that this story took place, which must have been shortly before the War, had been a good one for rice production. When the harvest came, Captain Ward placed John in charge of the threshing floor just in front of the rice barn. John worked under the direction of Devine, the Driver or head slave, and under the direction of the white Overseer of course, but Captain Ward trusted John completely and gave him serious responsibilities. After all, John was the Class Leader on Brookgreen Plantation.

The harvest was in full swing. Every day rice flats piled high with bundles of rice stalks laden with plump grains of rice arrived at Brookgreen Landing, just down the rice island steps from us here at the Museum. A steady stream of field hands carried bundles of rice stalks up the steps from flatboats to the barnyard. John directed them as they arranged the bundles on the hard packed dirt of the threshing floor in front of the barn.

Under John's supervision, workers beat the rice stalks with wooden flails to knock rice grains loose from the stalks. Then, they scooped up the rough rice from the threshing floor into coiled seagrass baskets and carried it into the rice barn to storage bins where it would wait for milling later in the season. Finally, they carried off the bundles of rice stalks, now just the remaining straw, to an outbuilding for storage.

At least, that was what was supposed to happen. But now the Overseer had discovered that John wasn't sending all the rice into the barn. There in the dark of the midnight barnyard the Overseer had discovered the secret of John's thievery!

~   ~   ~

The Overseer was eager to tell Captain Ward what he had discovered, especially since it involved John, whom he had long suspected of being less perfect than Captain Ward believed. The Overseer went to Captain Ward first thing the next morning and recounted his story.

Captain Ward was a strict man but he was fair. When his Overseer came to him with the story of John leading other field hands in stealing rice, Captain Ward determined to give John a chance to defend himself against the charge. Stealing was a serious offense that merited severe punishment.

Captain Ward sent for John. There on the front porch of the plantation mansion that stood where the *Alligator Bender* Pool stands today, in the presence of the Ward family, the household servants, and the Overseer, Captain Ward confronted his trusted Class Leader.

"John, are you a good Christian man?"

"I most certainly am, Master Josh, sir!" John replied with enthusiasm.

Captain Ward agreed and went on to praise John's leadership and his fine record of behavior and hard work at Brookgreen. Then he grew more solemn.

"John, I need to ask you about something and I'm sure you will tell me the truth. You know it is a sin to lie."

"Most certainly, Master Josh, sir," John agreed.

Captain Ward went on to detail the Overseer's charges. He concluded with a direct question, "John, are you stealing my rice?"

Shocked, John drew himself up to his full height and looked Captain Ward straight in the eye.

"Stealing! I am not stealing!" John exclaimed! His exact words, in the Gullah language that he had spoken all his life, were "T'ief! Ah don't t'ief!"

"Master Josh, sir," John went on to explain, "The rice is your property, isn't it, sir?"

To this Captain Ward readily agreed.

"And I am your property, and all of us slaves are your property, aren't we, sir?"

Again, Captain Ward agreed.

"Now how is it stealing?" John asked, staring earnestly at his master. "When we move your rice from your barnyard into your slaves, we are just moving one property into another property. You haven't lost any property. It's still your rice and your slaves."

Captain Ward stared at John but had no answer for him.

Miss Bessie, Captain Ward's wife, spoke up quickly in support of John. "That's right!" she proclaimed emphatically with an amused smile, "My rice, my slaves!"

Captain Ward was never sure whether John was too clever for him in his use of words, or whether John was truly sincere in his understanding of the economics of the situation. Either way, Captain Ward felt compelled to forego any punishment for taking the rice. However, in the future he did keep a much closer eye on his most trusted worker: John, the Class Leader of Brookgreen Plantation!

That wasn't quite the end of the story though. In front of the whole group gathered there on the porch that morning, Miss Bessie went on to insist that if workers were taking extra rice, it was because they weren't getting enough to eat. With another smile she ordered the Overseer to increase their weekly rations!

And over the years Miss Bessie always broke into that same smile as she recalled Captain Ward's consternation on the mansion porch that morning.

"My rice, my slaves!" she always repeated, chuckling to herself whenever she told the story, as she often did in years to come.

"My rice, my slaves!"

The White Lady of the Hermitage

"What can you tell us about the ghost of Alice Flagg?" a curious visitor asked Miss Genevieve one sweltering afternoon. Miss Genevieve rarely told this story in my hearing. Perhaps she considered it her brother's story, as he still lived in Alice's home. But when asked, she certainly complied.

When I first came to this area with my parents, Mr. and Mrs. Clarke Wilcox Sr., in the early part of this century, we lived in a house called the Hermitage on the creek at Murrells Inlet. Some say it was built in the 1840s by Dr. Allard Belin Flagg, one of the grandsons of Rachel Moore Allston Flagg who entertained both Lord Cornwallis and President Washington here as the Mistress of Brookgreen (you remember her). Others say the Hermitage was built even earlier. Whatever its age, local people far and near declared to us that the Hermitage was haunted and had been for generations. And they were right. We came to know our resident ghost as a lovely and harmless apparition. We always called her the White Lady but my brother Clarke has done some research and says she is Alice Flagg.

In the mid-1800s Dr. Allard Belin Flagg (really "II," because he had had an older brother of the same name who died as an infant, although no one ever used the "II" but called him "Dr. Allard" to distinguish him from the many other Flagg relatives who were physicians) was the owner of Wachesaw Plantation, just up the Waccamaw Neck from Brookgreen. In those days rice plantations along the Waccamaw River were the richest in the world. Rice planters considered themselves the aristocracy of the nation.

Like most rice plantations on the Waccamaw Neck, Wachesaw Plantation was narrow in the north-south direction but wide in the east-west direction. It stretched from low and swampy rice fields along the Waccamaw River, through higher pine lands, to the cool breezes of the seashore at Murrells Inlet, and on over to the sandy beaches of Flagg's Landing, which we call Garden City Beach nowadays.

Dr. Allard built his home on a point of land surrounded by the saltwater creeks and marshes of Murrells Inlet. (By the way, the "creek" is the saltwater channel through the marsh that fills with ocean water twice a day as the tides rise and fall.) There, shaded by ancient live oaks hung with moss, surrounded by thickets of myrtle and sweet bay, Dr. Allard escaped the heat and pestilence of his swampy rice fields. Because of the much-desired solitude it provided him, Dr. Allard named his home the Hermitage.

Although most homes on the seashore were merely summer retreats, the Hermitage was large and gracious, especially by today's standards. Rooms downstairs were light and airy with high ceilings and lovely polished pine floors. Upstairs bedrooms had lots of windows for cross ventilation. A large front porch facing the water caught sea breezes and afforded an ever-changing view of creeks and marshes that stretch to the two barrier islands of Flagg's Landing and Magnolia Beach, separated by the narrow mouth of the inlet, and of vessels of all sorts that wound their way through those creeks, as they had for centuries.

Later in life Dr. Allard married and raised a family (Miss Dusenbury can tell you more about various members of his family another time. All of these stories are connected, don't you know!), but at the time of this story he was still a bachelor. Dr. Allard's widowed mother, Margaret Belin Flagg, and his younger sister, Alice, lived with him in the Hermitage under his support and protection.

Life at the Hermitage was isolated and sometimes lonely for Alice as she entered her teenage years. Although she loved the creatures of the creeks and marshes and the flowers and birds of the surrounding forests, she longed for human companionship. Sometimes Alice accompanied her mother on visits to relatives in other parts of the state that lasted several weeks, or on shopping trips to Georgetown or Charleston that lasted several days.

The family occasionally visited in other plantation homes on the Waccamaw Neck. On Sundays they often traveled down the Waccamaw River to attend services at All Saints Episcopal Church near Pawley's Island. These were delightful day-long outings when Alice could socialize with young people from other aristocratic planter families who attended the services. Other Sundays the family remained at home and Dr. Allard simply read passages from his prayer book to the family and servants in his stern and somber voice.

No one can tell us exactly where and how Alice met her young man. That part of the story has not come down to us. Her family certainly did not arrange the meeting!

Now, this young man was handsome and healthy. He was educated, honest, and financially successful. But he was an Horry (pronounced "O-REE") County turpentine operator and therefore not of the rice planter social class.

Horry County, the county just north of Brookgreen's Georgetown County, produced many such men in the 1800s. Horry's vast pine forests yielded timber as well as turpentine and other naval stores, such as pitch and tar, vital to building and maintaining ships. Fortunes were made in naval stores and timber shipped down the Waccamaw River from Horry County to world-wide markets. But these fortunes were paltry compared to the wealth of rice planters here in Georgetown County. Here, geography allowed for the raising of "Carolina Gold," the long grain rice first discovered and grown right here on Brookgreen Plantation by old Colonel Joshua John Ward, Dr. Allard's future father-in-law.

By Dr. Allard's time, rice had been the source of fabulous wealth for the Georgetown County planters for one hundred and fifty years. Georgetown County rice planters dined off fine English porcelain and drank imported wines from French crystal glassware. They educated their sons in England and Europe. Their elegant wives and daughters, arrayed in their finest silks and delicate satins, entertained visitors in the ballrooms and libraries of their Georgetown County plantation mansions.

In contrast, the "ladies" of Conwayborough, Horry County's courthouse town and largest community, were best known for smoking corncob pipes.

So, through some accident, Alice met and fell in love with a handsome young turpentine operator from Horry County. Some have even suggested that this young man could have been one of Miss Dusenbury's grandfathers! Both of them were handsome and successful young turpentine operators in Horry County at that time.

Whoever he was, the relationship between Alice and her young turpentine operator grew, in spite of Dr. Allard's attempts to discourage the romance. Evidently he was wise enough not to forbid contact with the "undesirable" young suitor completely.

In fact, one story tells of the young suitor appearing at the Hermitage one afternoon in a fancy buggy pulled by a beautiful bay mare. He formally requested Dr. Allard's permission to take Miss Alice for a drive along the narrow trail known as the King's Highway, which passed close to the Hermitage. Dr. Allard readily acquiesced in an equally polite and formal manner. Then, while the young suitor waited, Dr. Allard had his own horse saddled. Next, he escorted Alice out of the Hermitage and helped her into the buggy, climbing up beside her himself. Finally, he indicated to the young suitor that he might ride the saddled horse alongside the buggy and converse with Miss Alice while he, Dr. Allard, drove his sister along the shore road. And so the courtship proceeded.

As fall approached, Dr. Allard and his mother decided that the time had come to send Alice to Charleston to complete her education. It was also time to introduce her into society. In Charleston Alice would meet sons of other rice planters from whom she would eventually select her husband. The marriage would no doubt continue the tradition of alliances among Lowcountry planters that had kept lands and fortunes secure among a select few aristocratic families for the previous centuries.

Sending Alice to Charleston would have the added benefit of separating her from her undesirable suitor. Dr. Allard and his mother hoped that Alice would forget her childish infatuation with the turpentine operator once she was among her school companions and engaged in Charleston's never-ending whirl of social activities.

Alice was excited about the prospect of going to school in Charleston but her heart belonged to her beloved young man from Horry County! They arranged one last meeting before Alice's departure. There, under ancient live oaks along the shore, they pledged their love to each other. Both hoped that when Alice returned from Charleston the next summer and Dr. Allard saw that their feelings for each other remained strong, he would relent. If not, they would simply wait until Alice was old enough to marry without her family's consent.

There along the creek, the young man presented Alice with a simple gold ring as a token of his love. They both understood that Alice would be unable to wear the ring,due to her family's disapproval. But Alice would have a special keepsake during their long separation.

Under the oaks they embraced one last time, and perhaps even kissed, although times were quite different then than now. Finally they parted.

Charleston was an exciting city for Alice who was a beautiful, refined, and quite wealthy young woman. We know nothing of the school she attended or the details of her social life but we can imagine.

Perhaps Alice attended Madame Talavande's School for Girls on Legare Street. Madame Talavande only took girls from the best families. She taught them French and music along with the social graces. Most importantly, Madame Talavande guaranteed close supervision of her pupils as they became polished young ladies. She had had a high brick wall built around her school after the unfortunate elopement of one of her charges several years earlier. She had even purchased an elaborate wrought iron gate depicting crossed swords and spears for the front entrance, designed to discourage unwanted visitors. The Sword Gate and high brick wall still protect her house today. (So does Madame Talavande's ghost but that's another story.)

Alice's social life in Charleston was a whirlwind of teas, suppers, concerts, and balls, all carefully supervised of course. Race Week in February brought together society from all the best families, as did St. Cecilia's Ball, the culmination of the social season. Alice delighted in the attention she received from dashing young men who flocked around her at every opportunity. However, her heart remained true to her young suitor from the turpentine forests. She always wore his ring on a thin satin ribbon around her neck. The ribbon was just long enough to allow the ring to rest over her heart, and to conceal it beneath her modest gown.

Still, Alice may have shared her story with her closest schoolmates. A secret love waiting for her in the wilds of Horry would have made a wonderfully romantic tale when moonlight filtered into darkened sleeping rooms at Madame Talavande's.

And so the long months passed. But with the coming of spring, and the prospect of returning home, also came illness. Fevers of all types had always been common in the Carolina Lowcountry. Alice's fevers grew worse and worse until finally the school sent a message to her family to come for Alice, as they could no longer care for her. Alice's mother was away visiting relatives but Dr. Allard arrived to take his ill sister home.

Their trip took several days: by coastal schooner to Georgetown, then by plantation boat across the bay and up the Waccamaw River to Wachesaw Landing, and finally by buggy across the Waccamaw Neck to the Hermitage. Throughout the journey Alice grew steadily weaker.

Once she arrived home, loving servants carried Alice upstairs to her bedroom overlooking the creek. She was delirious with fever as they placed her in her own soft bed. There, as they arranged the bedclothes, the plain gold ring on its slim satin ribbon slipped into sight.

Dr. Allard stared coldly at the ring. Slowly he removed it from around his sister's pale neck. Alice, again lucid but too weak to stop him, began to beg for the return of her precious ring, a present from her own true love.

As Alice pleaded with Dr. Allard, fury overtook him! Alice had persisted in her attachment to that unworthy youth! She had even accepted a ring from him!

Overcome by anger, Dr. Allard flung the ring through an open window toward the marsh with all his might! Alice's eyes and heart followed the ring in its flight but her body was worn out by pleading. She sank back into delirium.

Dr. Allard's fury subsided as he watched his frail sister suffer. He and the household servants remained with her throughout the night. At times she roused, pleading frantically for the return of her precious ring. At other times she seemed to sleep peacefully. But by daylight Alice was gone, another victim of Lowcountry fevers.

Alice's mother was still absent but burial could not be delayed in the increasing heat. Servants dressed Alice in her beautiful white gown from the St. Cecilia's Ball and arranged her lovingly on satin pillows in her finely crafted coffin. They laid her to rest temporarily in an earthen bank along the shore near the home of her uncle, James Belin, the local Methodist minister. Parson Belin spoke a few simple words over her temporary resting place as they covered it with white oyster shells.

Later when her mother returned, the family moved Alice's body to the cemetery at All Saints Church and Reverend Glennie held the proper Episcopal funeral. One wonders if among the numerous planters and their families stood one lone mourner, somewhat out of place, a handsome young man, obviously well-to-do but clearly not "one-of-us," who lingered under the live oaks in the church yard cemetery long after all others had left, saying good-bye to his one true love.

Alice's grave can still be seen in All Saints Cemetery to this day. A marble slab engraved with only the name

"Alice" covers it. Some people claim Alice can be seen there, too. There are lots of stories about it, and some silliness about walking around her grave thirteen times backward at midnight. It seems like a lot of work to summon a ghost but there is a pathway worn around the grave so people must try it.

At the Hermitage where my brother Clarke still lives, our White Lady comes and goes as she pleases, not at anyone's beck and call. Perhaps she is still looking for her lost ring. Some have seen her walking near the shell-covered bank that was her temporary resting place or along the shore closer to the Hermitage. Miss Dusenbury has seen her there.

At Miss Genevieve's bidding, Cousin Corrie took up the story . . .

One evening at dusk my younger sister Dell and I walked over to the Hermitage to visit the Wilcox family. We were sitting on the front porch enjoying the sea breeze and waiting for Mr. and Mrs. Wilcox, Mrs. Chandler and her husband, and Mrs. Chandler's brothers, Charlie and Dick, to finish eating supper. Suddenly the two Wilcox dogs that had been sleeping at our feet jumped up, growled, and scooted inside! We looked out and saw a glowing patch of light in the yard toward the water. At that point we followed the dogs inside! When we all returned to investigate, the light patch was gone. Perhaps it had just been the lamp shining through the dining room window but we asked ourselves, "What about the dogs?"

Miss Genevieve continued . . .

Most often, the White Lady appears in Alice's upstairs bedroom, which my parents always used as a guest room. My brother Dick has seen her there a number of times and even walked right through her once. A little cousin staying in Alice's bedroom one time described a beautiful Lady in White who had comforted him when he was crying. My mother's sister occasionally saw her there in the dressing table mirror and finally told us that if we kept putting her in that bedroom to sleep, she would stop visiting us! She was tired of being startled by the apparition.

My mother started to sleep in Alice's bedroom one night herself. She was tired from working in the flower garden all day and my father had wanted to read in bed so my mother moved across the hall to the guest room for a good night's sleep. As she lay there in the dark, planning what she wanted to do with the flowerbeds the next day, she was surprised to see the securely latched door swing open. Then she saw a luminous white cloud the size and shape of a person glide into the room and out again. She doesn't sleep in there anymore, either!

But in spite of being startled, we have always enjoyed our ghost. She is quite one of the family.

Cousin Corrie spoke up again with a smile, "Yes, you do enjoy your ghost! Your mother, Mrs. Wilcox, told me a story years ago about your fun with the White Lady . . ."

Before we had electricity at the Inlet we all lit our homes with kerosene lamps. One night, shortly after Mrs. Chandler and her husband were married, they were relaxing in the downstairs sitting room of the Hermitage. It was lit by a kerosene lamp. Mrs. Wilcox needed the light somewhere else briefly so Mrs. Chandler, here, picked up the lamp and carried it off to her mother, leaving her husband sitting peacefully in the dark. Pretty soon a cry arose from the darkened sitting room, "Bring back the lamp!"

When Mrs. Wilcox and Mrs. Chandler hurried back with the lamp, they found Mr. Chandler sitting stiffly with eyes as big as saucers. He said that "someone" had been in the room with him but "she" had floated out into the hall and up the stairs.

Excited and a little alarmed, they decided to investigate. Mrs. Wilcox told Mr. Chandler to take the lamp and go first. She would follow and Mrs. Chandler would bring up the rear. (Mrs. Wilcox told me that her main objective was to get safely between the two of them!) So they went out of the sitting room and into the hall in that order, with Mr. Chandler in the lead holding the lamp way up over his head.

As they entered the hall they passed Mrs. Wilcox's sewing basket sitting on the Victrola. It contained a pair of soft pajamas waiting to be mended. In a spirit of mischief, Mrs. Chandler, here, grabbed up the pajamas, wadded them into a ball, and threw them up into the air over the stairs. She was so quick that all anyone saw was this white *thing* unfolding and coming down the stairs at them! Mrs. Wilcox said that she gave one screech so loud that it scared the neighbors, and then they all laughed until they nearly "gave up the ghost" themselves.

Ghost Ships

Both Cousin Corrie and Miss Genevieve were members of Belin Memorial Methodist Church in Murrells Inlet. One day Miss Genevieve and Cousin Corrie offered these thoughts as they talked about reports of strange visions from the church steps. I always believed both ladies leaned toward Confederate block-ade runners as the origin of the ghostly wrecks. Cousin Corrie began the story . . .

Some people have seen ghostly apparitions from the steps of our Methodist Church at Murrells Inlet. At certain times, wrecked sailing vessels appear out in the creek or at the mouth of the inlet between Garden City and Huntington Beach where real sailing vessels used to come and go. Dawn and dusk seem to be the most common times to see them. Hulls, rigging, and masts, sometimes remains of small boats and sometimes remains of larger ships, have appeared, always far out in the marsh. Certain wrecks have even reappeared from time to time in the same location. Nothing is found when anyone explores the locations in full daylight however. And people only see the wrecks when they look out from our church porch steps.

I've never seen any of the ghost ships myself and no one has been able to say exactly what these vessels might be. Surely some are simply present-day pleasure craft ca-reening on their sides, caught in the creek by low tide until rising water floats them again. Others are harder to ex-plain, and there are so many possibilities.

Our creeks and inlets have seen so many vessels over the centuries. The first inhabitants used dugout canoes to gather the rich sea life. Then, in succession, came Spanish explorers in barques and sloops looking for safe harbors, English pirates seeking fresh water and food or looking for spots to hide their booty, British raiders intent on destroying Patriot salt works, Confederate blockade runners bringing in medicines or weapons and carrying out cotton, rice, and naval stores, as well as Yankee warships shelling inland plantations or landing troops to skirmish with local coastal defenses. More recently, Prohibition rumrunners landed contraband from Cuba. In between came passenger vessels, cargo ships, and private yachts seeking shelter from Atlantic storms. And fishermen of all eras have always harvested the teeming waters.

These ghostly wrecks could represent any era or any story. They could be relics of man's unsuccessful struggles with the powers of Nature or the remains of battles fought between human adversaries.

Why do we see these ghost ships only from the Methodist Church? Perhaps clues lie in its history, really three different histories that come together here in one location. At Belin Memorial Methodist Church we have the history of the land, the church building, and the church steps, each tinged with its own ghostly associations.

~   ~   ~

The land where our church stands has long been known for its supernatural connections. It was part of Wachesaw Plantation, acquired by Parson James Belin, a Methodist minister here in the early 1800s (you remember him). Francis Asbury, the first Bishop of the Methodist Church in America, who used to travel these parts on horseback, ordained Parson Belin.

Parson Belin built a sturdy home for himself on the seacoast at Murrells Inlet out of hand-hewn timbers from his own land. Wooden pegs held the timbers and boards together. The house's several large rooms have sheltered numerous families over the years and the "Old Methodist Parsonage" still stands today as the oldest building in Murrells Inlet.

Parson Belin called his home "Cedar Hill" because of the thick growth of cedars in that area back in his day. The point of land where his home stood became known as Parsonage Point and the channel in front of his home is still called Parsonage Creek today.

Methodism was slow to catch on in Georgetown County where the Episcopal Church, successor to the Church of England, was firmly established. Slave owning rice planters preferred Episcopal teachings that slavery was acceptable in the sight of God to the tenets of Methodism, which at first opposed slavery. Methodists were more successful at converting followers in neighboring Horry County where the more independent and less wealthy small farmers owned few, if any, slaves.

As you may recall, while Parson Belin found few converts to Methodism among rice planters, these planters did encourage his missionary work among their slaves. Parson Belin began preaching and teaching Christianity to slaves on his own Wachesaw Plantation as well as to those on neighboring Brookgreen and Springfield Plantations, two of the plantations that later became Brookgreen Gardens. He continued and expanded his Mission to the Slaves for many years. He also served small congregations of both white and black members at Turkey Hill Plantation (just south of Brookgreen Gardens) and at Socastee (a settlement a few miles to the west) and Murrells Inlet where he lived. He even traveled to preach at small churches such as Hebron Methodist Church in Horry County where he happened to have baptized my grandmother, Fannie Sarvis.

Just before the War Between the States, after many years of devoted service, Parson Belin fell from his buggy one evening when he was all alone. He died right there in his own yard. Parson Belin left a long elaborate will including the bequest of his home at Cedar Hill, and one hundred acres surrounding it, to the Methodist Church. This is the land where our Methodist Church stands today. The circumstances of his death were somewhat mysterious and some say his ghost still walks this shore.

It was also at Cedar Hill that Parson Belin's lovely niece, Alice Flagg, who had lived at the Hermitage on another part of Wachesaw Plantation, was first interred after her tragic death. Her ghost is sometimes seen walking along this seashore, perhaps looking for her lost ring (but you've already heard that story from Miss Genevieve).

Supernatural beings of Gullah folklore also frequent Parsonage Point. Local people have long reported difficulties with fearsome haunts and spectral creatures when passing the Cedar Hill area at night. One local woman often talked to Miss Genevieve about her frightening encounter there with a fearsome plat-eye (but that's another story).

So perhaps the ghostly wrecks out in the creek have some connection to this land that Parson Belin bequeathed to the Methodist Church, or to Parson Belin who cannot rest in peace, or to the ghostly Alice who was once buried along this shore, or even to the spirit world of the Gullah that remains so alive right here.

~   ~   ~

However, some believe it is more likely that the ghostly ships have a connection to the church building itself rather than to the land. This building does have an interesting history of its own, a history that also began with Parson Belin but in an entirely different location.

As Parson Belin became known for his missionary work on the Waccamaw Neck, other planters began to support his efforts. The Pyatt family of Turkey Hill Plantation, just south of Brookgreen Gardens, built a church for Parson Belin's congregation of worshipers in their area. The church was a simple rectangular building made of hand-hewn timbers set on a foundation of brick pillars that elevated it several feet above the sandy ground. Four wooden columns held up the front porch roof.

Parson Belin often preached in Turkey Hill Church to slaves as well as to the few white Methodist families on that part of the Waccamaw Neck. These white Methodists would have been families of plantation overseers, seafaring men, or other workingmen. The elite planters themselves all attended All Saints Episcopal Church close to Pawley's Island.

After Parson Belin's death, circuit riding Methodist preachers continued to serve Turkey Hill Church, but when the slaves were freed they established their own churches, leaving just a white congregation. Over the years, membership at Turkey Hill Church dwindled until by 1925 there were only two families left attending the infrequent services. That year Mrs. Oliver, whose family owned a restaurant and fishing retreat called Oliver's Lodge on Parsonage Point in Murrells Inlet, convinced the two remaining families to donate the Turkey Hill Church building to be moved to Parsonage Point and placed on the land that Parson Belin had bequeathed to the Methodist Church.

Mrs. Oliver enlisted Captain Boo Lachicotte, who ran a caviar and smoked sturgeon operation near Litchfield Plantation (and was a grandson of the first rice mill engineer at Brookgreen Plantation), to take the church apart into movable sections and transport it to Parsonage Point in his wagons pulled by strong mules. It must have been quite a sight as parts of the church building slowly traveled up the King's Highway! In pieces, Parson Belin's church left Turkey Hill Plantation, passed through The Oaks, Brookgreen, Springfield, and Laurel Hill, the four plantations that became Brookgreen Gardens, and finally arrived at its new resting place on what had been Wachesaw Plantation! Its brick pillars were so solid that Captain Boo transported them intact and used them as the foundation again in the new location.

Turkey Hill Church had withstood hurricanes and war for over a century. What lives had passed through its doors? What dramas had its members and visitors, both black and white, played out over the years? What spirits were disturbed as Captain Boo began to dismantle the ancient church building? Miss Genevieve, here, can give you one answer.

Miss Genevieve took up the tale . . .

Stories of those uneasy spirits began to circulate among the local people as Captain Boo began his work. Perhaps some of those stories were in the minds of those helping dismantle the church as work proceeded one dark and stormy morning. Suddenly a strange noise became noticeable. A faint humming seemed to come from the very air around the front of the church!

My husband, Tom Chandler, was one of those helping move the building. He had always been sensitive to the spirit world and said that he began to have a shivery feeling between his shoulder blades as the hum grew louder and louder. Several workers glanced sideways at each other and at the partially dismantled building as they made excuses to leave.

Was this a warning from Beyond? The braver, or more foolish, ones, including Tom, gradually began to investigate. They finally discovered the earthly source of the unearthly hum: their work had disturbed a colony of honeybees long resident inside one of the front porch columns. Closer examination showed that each of the four columns was packed with honeycomb and bees!

The workers decided that it would be easier to build new columns for the porch once it was in place at Parsonage Point than to clean out and transport the old ones, so they left that part of the church building at Turkey Hill. They did manage to harvest much of the delicious honey and comb, taking the unexpected treat home to their families along with the story of the spirit humming.

Cousin Corrie continued . . .

So Parson Belin's Turkey Hill Church became Belin Memorial Methodist Church on Parsonage Point. It is possible that the ghostly wrecks in the Inlet have some connection to people who used the church building in its previous life at Turkey Hill, people who came and went and sometimes lost their lives and fortunes in shipwrecks on creeks and rivers and oceans in the Lowcountry.

~   ~   ~

But those who talk of ghostly wrecks have usually seen them only from the church porch steps. And these porch steps, strangely enough, have their own separate history.

Travel on the Waccamaw Neck in the 1800s was difficult at best. The river served as the main thoroughfare as progress overland along the primitive King's Highway was slow and tiresome. But travel on the river also required much effort as well as careful timing to take advantage of tidal flows.

The Church of England, and then, after the American Revolution, the Episcopal Church, designated all of the thirty-mile-long Waccamaw Neck as All Saints Parish. Rice planters had originally built the parish church inland from Pawley's Island on land donated by Thomas Pawley, one of the early planters. It was about in the middle of the Waccamaw Neck, just five miles south of Brookgreen Gardens. All Saints Church, now in its fourth incarnation, has a long and interesting history (but that's another story). The point is that it was hard for planters and their families living on the northern and southern extremes of the Waccamaw Neck to get to All Saints Church regularly for services.

Planters solved this problem by building small chapels on their own plantations where their families and servants gathered for Sunday services most weeks, in between their less frequent visits to services at All Saints Church. Sometimes several planters got together to build a "chapel-of-ease" to be shared by all families in an area. The minister of All Saints Church occasionally visited these chapels but often planters themselves conducted services.

One such chapel-of-ease, called St. John-the-Evangelist Chapel, was built in a grove of trees overlooking the Waccamaw River on Wachesaw Plantation a few miles north of Brookgreen Gardens. Some say Dr. Allard Flagg of the Hermitage, a grandson of Rachel Moore Allston Flagg and Dr. Henry Flagg of Brookgreen Plantation, built St. John-the-Evangelist Chapel shortly before the War Between the States. Others say it was much older.

Although the chapel was simple, it was made of the finest heartwood pine and cypress. Six sandstone slabs brought by ship from England, three for the front, two for the side, and one for the back, served as steps for the small chapel. By 1860, planters and their servants from the

68

northern part of the Waccamaw Neck and those from Sandy Island behind Brookgreen Gardens as well as seafaring folk from Murrells Inlet were all attending services regularly at St. John-the-Evangelist Chapel.

When the War came, the United States Navy made ending Confederate trade with the rest of the world its primary mission. The South Atlantic Blockading Squadron under the command of Admiral John Dahlgren began forming naval blockades around all main southern ports to keep ships of any type from going in or out. Of course, daring ship captains like the dashing Rhett Butler in *Gone with the Wind*, whether motivated by patriotism for the Southern Cause or financial rewards of trading in valuable commodities, immediately began running the blockade.

Early in the War, most blockade runners slipped into larger ports such as Charleston and Georgetown here in South Carolina or Wilmington up in North Carolina. However by the middle of the War, Union gunboats had successfully blockaded all larger southern ports. Smaller ports became the lifeblood of the Confederacy. Confederate blockade runners began operating out of Murrells Inlet, risking, and sometimes losing, their lives and vessels in attempts to keep Confederate trade with the rest of the world open.

Confederate Trade Routes

Quite elaborate trade routes developed along long, intricate, and often arduous pathways for vital commodities heading to or from blockade runners at Murrells Inlet. Wachesaw Landing, on the Waccamaw River just across the Waccamaw Neck from Murrells Inlet, became the gathering point for goods from all over this part of the state.

Rice produced on plantations along the lower Waccamaw River was loaded onto flats and rowed or poled upstream to Wachesaw Landing. Rice from plantations along the lower Pee Dee River farther inland was loaded onto flats that were first floated down the Pee Dee to Winyah Bay, then rowed over to the mouth of the Waccamaw, and from there, rowed or poled upstream to Wachesaw Landing. These were simple routes but ones that required substantial effort.

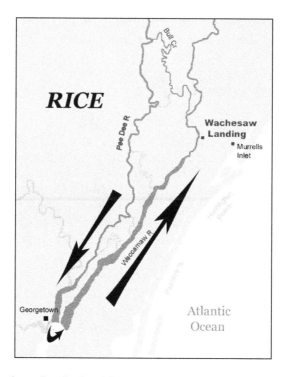

Flats loaded with timber or naval stores, mainly pitch and tar, from the upper Waccamaw River floated downriver to Wachesaw Landing directly and much more easily. Flats carrying the same materials from the upper Pee Dee River took an equally easy but more complicated route. First they floated fifty or sixty miles down the Pee Dee River to just past where it enters Georgetown County.

At that point, the Pee Dee and the Waccamaw Rivers begin to flow parallel to each other only a mile or so apart for their remaining fifteen miles until they empty into Winyah Bay near Georgetown. Several small creeks criss-cross the swamps between them, interconnecting the two rivers in an intricate web.

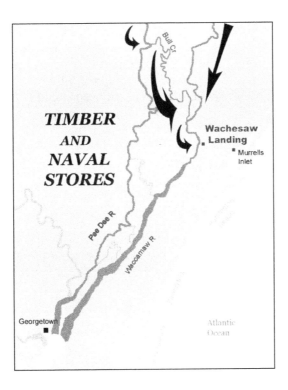

Twisty-turney Bull Creek actually carries a substantial amount of water from the Pee Dee River through the cypress swamps and into the Waccamaw River at Longwood Plantation (once owned by my Cousin Jack Green, often called "Drunken Jack," but that's another story).

So flats and barges loaded with timber and naval stores that had floated down from the upper Pee Dee River could easily cut across through Bull Creek over to the Wac-camaw River and then float on down the Waccamaw the rest of the way to Wachesaw Landing.

Cotton from inland plantations in South Carolina took a similar but even more elaborate route. First it trav-eled by railroad car from inland gathering points to a railroad bridge over the upper Pee Dee River near Cheraw, South Carolina. There it was transferred from railroad cars to river flats and barges. Then the cotton floated sixty miles down the Pee Dee River to the Bull Creek cut off, headed through the swamps on Bull Creek over to the Waccamaw River, and then continued on down the Waccamaw River to Wachesaw Landing.

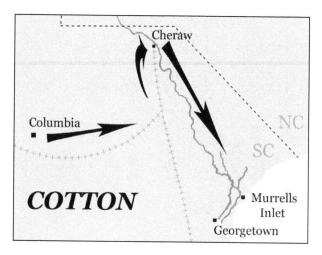

So by all these routes, cotton from inland planta-tions, naval stores and timber from the upper Waccamaw and Pee Dee Rivers, and rice from the lower Waccamaw and Pee Dee Rivers all converged on Wachesaw Landing.

At Wachesaw Landing workers unloaded all these cargos from river flats and barges and piled them onto ox-drawn wagons that carried them the three miles across the Waccamaw Neck to Murrells Inlet.

At Murrells Inlet the various cargoes were loaded onto ocean-going schooners, which ran the blockade and headed for Europe or the Caribbean. There their captains sold the valuable cotton, rice, naval stores, and timber, then used the money to purchase even more precious weapons and medicines vital to the Confederacy.

Returning schooner captains then ran their ships back through the Union blockade to bring these precious goods into Murrells Inlet. Workers then transferred this cargo from ships to the ox-drawn wagons and carted it across the Waccamaw Neck to Wachesaw Landing. From there the goods traveled on to their final destinations, following the various original pathways but in reverse.

We can imagine handsome and daring young blockade runners waiting at Murrells Inlet for their ships to be loaded with valuable commodities from throughout the state. Local planter families, coastal merchants, and traders (only the highest type of course) would have welcomed them to Sunday services at St. John-the-Evangelist Chapel and applauded them for their daring feats in support of the Cause.

Perhaps the dashing blockade runners lingered on the stone steps of St. John-the-Evangelist after services, exchanging news of the War with local men and pleasantries with their lovely daughters. These young men were heroes, celebrated in the desperate struggle for Southern

Independence. Many a young lady's heart (and possibly several older ones) fluttered when one of these young heroes smiled her way. Old men shook their hands warmly and wished them Godspeed on their dangerous missions. Young boys followed them eagerly and dreamed of being old enough to take the helm of sea-going schooners. No young men wished them well there on St. John-the-Evangelist Chapel's steps however; all the young men were off fighting in Tennessee or Virginia.

Bonds formed quickly in wartime between daring blockade runners and the people of the Waccamaw Neck. When these young heroes made their way out through inlet creeks, the hearts of local residents sailed with them.

At first blockade runners moved easily in and out of Murrells Inlet delivering load after load of goods to foreign buyers. For a while, in the middle of the War, a fully loaded schooner sailed from Murrells Inlet almost every day.

However in 1863 events turned disastrous for blockade runners operating out of Murrells Inlet. Admiral Dahlgren, Commander of the South Atlantic Blockading Squadron, was determined to shut off all flow of trade to the South. With larger ports successfully blockaded, he ordered the Union Navy to turn its attention to smaller ports. Federal gunboats attacked inside Murrells Inlet, sinking or burning ship after ship throughout the summer and fall of that year. Shelling destroyed five schooners loaded with cotton on one single day here, but ships still continued to slip in and out of Murrells Inlet regularly.

Admiral Dahlgren became so angry at the success of our blockade runners that he organized a special expedition to attack Murrells Inlet in December of 1863. The attack was not particularly successful because winter storms disrupted its efforts but on New Year's Eve the expedition did manage to set fire to a schooner docked at Murrells Inlet fully loaded with turpentine. Residents long remembered the resulting blaze that "turned night into day" along the seashore.

In spite of spotty success, attacks on Murrells Inlet continued steadily. By the spring of 1864 Admiral Dahlgren had accomplished his goal. Burned hulls, broken masts, and torn rigging littered creeks from the mouth of Murrells Inlet all the way to the shore. Finally, the rapidly failing Confederacy abandoned Murrells Inlet as a port, and then abandoned the whole of the Waccamaw Neck to Federal troops. Admiral Dahlgren was able to celebrate his success, for a while at least (but that's still another story).

So, many think the ghostly wrecks they see from the steps of Belin Memorial Methodist Church are the sad remains of ships that carried those daring blockade runners. After visiting joyfully with local families on these steps of St. John-the-Evangelist Chapel, many lost their vessels, and sometimes their lives, in their doomed attempts to save a dying cause. Perhaps, sad and frightened residents of Murrells Inlet later lingered on these same steps comforting each other before entering the chapel to mourn the lost seamen and broken wrecks that represented the destruction of their hopes for their traditional way of life.

~   ~   ~

The War ended the plantation system. Once-wealthy All Saints Parish lost its minister and was so destitute that years passed before the parish could afford to hire another one. Even then he did not serve the small chapels. As at Turkey Hill, freed slaves soon organized their own churches. Remaining white families tried to keep the small chapels open but attendance declined. Attendance at St. John-the-Evangelist ceased entirely so this chapel-of-ease was abandoned and fell into disrepair.

Dr. Allard Flagg continued to operate Wachesaw Plantation after the War as best he could, now sharing the Hermitage with his wife and growing family. Rather than let the timbers and boards from the abandoned St. John-the-Evangelist Chapel go to waste, Dr. Allard decided to salvage them and use them to build a beach house for his family across the marsh at Flagg's Landing, today called Garden City Beach.

The Wachesaw Plantation owner had already had his workers construct a plank walkway on wooden pilings all the way across the marsh, with a gap at the main creek to let boats pass through of course. It stretched nearly a mile from the Hermitage to the sandy barrier island that formed the easternmost extent of his holdings. He and his family could walk along the planks out into the marsh, row across the gap at the main creek, and then continue on along the walkway through the marsh on the other side of the creek to reach the beach.

Dr. Allard directed his plantation workers to dismantle St. John-the-Evangelist Chapel carefully and haul the timbers and boards by wagon to the ocean-front spot he had selected for his beach house. Although his workers complied, there was much quiet muttering among them. It was not right to make a beach house out of church timbers! Still, the workers followed Dr. Allard's orders. They began framing the new house on the beach, but before they could complete the job, a September storm hit and blew it down.

This was a Sign, the workers agreed among themselves, but Dr. Allard directed them to gather up the scattered timbers and begin framing the house again. The muttering grew louder and more open but they still complied with his orders. They finished the framing and began siding the house. An October storm hit and blew the structure down once more. Another Sign!

Incredibly, Dr. Allard directed his workers to gather up the lumber and start framing the house a third time! Again most complied, although some workers refused at that point. Then a third storm hit and destroyed the building, this time scattering timbers and boards up and down the strand, here and gone. Finally, even Dr. Allard got the message. The Lord didn't want a beach house built with church timbers!

Miss Genevieve provided the conclusion of the story . . .

Although Dr. Allard tried to re-use timbers from St. John-the-Evangelist Chapel, he left the stone steps where they lay, never trying to include them in any other project. Perhaps he learned his lesson from the timbers.

Allard Belin Flagg died just after the turn of the century and the plantation passed out of family hands. Over the years, most folks forgot about St. John-the-Evangelist Chapel. Year by year, decade by decade, leaves and grasses covered the stone slabs in the deserted grove overlooking the Waccamaw River.

In 1910, my parents bought Wachesaw Plantation and we moved into the Hermitage. We had not only acquired a home but also its legacy of stories, secrets, and spirits. The stone steps of St. John-the-Evangelist were one of those secrets. Local people still living and working on the plantation led my parents to that lonely grove over-looking the Waccamaw River. As they told stories of St. John-the-Evangelist Chapel they scraped away layers of leaves to reveal the sandstone slabs hidden for so many years.

In 1925, when Mrs. Oliver had the Turkey Hill Church moved to Parsonage Point, my parents remem-bered the stone slabs at the site of St. John-the-Evangelist Chapel and donated them to be used as the steps for Belin

Memorial Methodist Church. Teams of oxen pulled them to their present location, which looks out over the Inlet marshes and creeks. Today, it is while standing on these stone steps that some people see skeletons of wrecked ships out in the marsh.

~   ~   ~

So these ghostly wrecks may have connections with the haunted land at Parsonage Point. They may have connections with Parson Belin's Turkey Hill Church building. Or they may have connections with the stone steps from St. John-the-Evangelist Chapel. No one knows but all agree that ghost ships always bring to mind the long, and often turbulent, history of our coast.

Ghost Ships

Brother Gator and His Friends

"Mrs. Chandler! Miss Dusenbury!" called the workman, rushing up the brick steps into the Museum almost out of breath. The Hostesses and I had just finished unlocking the post card display cases and the cash register to begin another day of welcoming visitors to Brookgreen Gardens.

"There's a six-foot alligator in the ladies' restroom! Don't go in there until we can get him out. We'll let you know as soon as it's safe!"

The workman hurried back to his task. I jumped up to follow him, as this sounded like the most exciting event of the summer!

Somehow the two elderly Hostesses did not share my enthusiasm for alligator chasing however, and I was quickly recalled to the safety of the Museum. Perhaps in compensation, or to distract me from further attempts to "help," Miss Genevieve began telling me stories of Brother Gator and his fellow inhabitants of the Waccamaw swamps.

Miss Genevieve had learned these stories from local people who lived on Sandy Island and along the seashore here at Brookgreen. Cousin Corrie and my own grandmother had heard similar stories as young children from family servants who told the stories in Gullah, a creole language of former slaves living along the South Carolina coast. Miss Genevieve collected these stories from the local people during the Depression as part of the federal government's WPA Writers' Project.

So that morning as I looked longingly through the open Museum window toward the ivy-covered wall that shaded the walkway to the ladies' restroom, Miss Genevieve told me how Brother Gator learned that there was Trouble in the world . . .

Brother Gator was a happy and trusting fellow. He enjoyed himself in the swamps all day long playing the fiddle and singing a happy song.

"Every day is good! Every day is good!" he sang.

He even played his fiddle for dances and to entertain his friends in the swamps, always singing the same song, "Every day is good! Every day is good!"

Brother Gator was so happy and trusting that his friends worried about him. They worried he did not understand the dangers and threats in the world well enough to take good care of himself. As much as they tried to make Brother Gator see dangers and problems, they could not convince him.

"Trouble?" Brother Gator would respond as he smiled his toothy smile, "What is Trouble? I've never seen any Trouble in my life."

He continued to fiddle and sing, "Every day is good! Every day is good!"

Brother Gator's friends finally decided that they had to do something to teach Brother Gator to see the world as it really is, for his own good of course.

One afternoon when Brother Gator had tired himself out fiddling and singing, he stretched out for a nap in the warm sun on a cushiony pile of dead reeds along the Waccamaw riverbank. As usual, he gave no thought to concealment or to possible danger.

Brother Rabbit saw his opportunity. As Brother Gator slept, Brother Rabbit ran to a nearby hearth and brought back a flaming ember, which was what local people used to start fires before matches were readily available. Round and round Brother Gator he scampered, lighting the dry reeds on fire. Soon flames encircled the sleeping alligator.

"Trouble!" yelled Brother Rabbit. "Trouble, Brother Gator, Trouble!"

As the flames closed in on him, Brother Gator awoke in a panic, feeling the heat all around him. "Oh no!" he cried. "This is **Trouble!**"

Luckily, alligators can move like lightening, especially when it is hot! So Brother Gator quickly escaped through the ring of fire into the river with only his toes and tail a little singed (although some say it was the heat of that fire that made his skin look cracked ever after).

Much to the relief of Brother Gator's friends, the lesson worked. From that day forward Brother Gator still enjoyed himself fiddling. He continued to play for dances and for his friends but he sang a new song.

"Some days are good! Some days are bad! Not every day is good!" sang Brother Gator.

And he was much more careful as he made his way through life, now that he knew that there was Trouble in the world.

Then Miss Genevieve told me how Brother Rabbit tried to trick Brother Frog out of some deer meat . . .

One summer Brother Rabbit and Brother Frog raised a garden together. Their vegetables grew large and lush because of their diligent work. Soon they had such an abundance of produce that they began discussing what to do with the extra.

Brother Rabbit thought of trading their vegetables for clothes but Brother Frog didn't want to do that because clothes would just get wet when he jumped into the pond. He suggested trading their vegetables for a horse but Brother Rabbit said he got around just fine on his own good legs. Finally they agreed that they would each like a hunting dog.

Brother Rabbit and Brother Frog knew that their neighbor, Mister Man, raised fine hunting dogs. They decided that each would trade some of his peas to Mister Man for a dog. So Brother Rabbit and Brother Frog each picked a bushel basket full of peas and set off together to see Mister Man.

As they walked along the sandy King's Highway, Brother Rabbit kept seeing Brother Frog swallowing and swallowing.

"Well if he can eat some of his peas, I can eat some of mine," thought Brother Rabbit, and he did.

Yet when Brother Rabbit and Brother Frog got to Mister Man's house, Brother Frog's basket was still full of peas.

"I thought you were swallowing peas!" cried Brother Rabbit.

"You foolish Rabbit," laughed Brother Frog. "Don't you know that frogs are always swallowing air?"

Brother Rabbit did feel foolish but he hid his embarrassment while they explained their desire to trade their peas for fine hunting dogs to their neighbor. This trade was agreeable to Mister Man, with one condition.

"Don't ever let me catch you using these dogs to hunt deer on my land," he warned, "or there will be the Devil to pay!"

Brother Rabbit and Brother Frog readily agreed to this condition and then commenced to bargaining.

Because Brother Frog's basket was full, Mister Man traded him a fine hunting dog for his peas. But Brother Rabbit's basket had short measure so the most Mister Man would give him for his peas was a runt pup, much to Brother Rabbit's disappointment, and to Brother Frog's amusement.

Their trading completed, the two friends started for home. Brother Frog, leading his fine hunting dog, was still laughing at Brother Rabbit for thinking that he had been swallowing his peas. Now he was also laughing at Brother Rabbit for having received only a runt pup in trade.

Brother Rabbit was none too happy about the situation. He didn't like Brother Frog laughing at him and he didn't like having only a runt pup, one he even had to carry because it was so puny. He kept looking out for a way to turn the tables on Brother Frog.

As Brother Frog and Brother Rabbit walked along through Mister Man's woods, a deer bounded across the road in front of them. Brother Frog's fine hunting dog immediately gave chase, with Brother Rabbit darting swiftly after him. Brother Frog hopped along behind as best he could.

Soon, deep in the woods, Brother Rabbit came upon a clearing where Brother Frog's dog had caught the deer and killed it. He quickly chased off the dog and set his runt pup on the deer.

Brother Frog finally arrived calling, "Look! My fine hunting dog caught the deer!"

"No!" Brother Rabbit cried. "My runt pup caught the deer!"

"What?" exclaimed Brother Frog! "A runt pup can't catch a deer!"

"Yes, my runt pup caught that deer! See, he's right there on him."

Brother Frog looked and looked and thought and thought. He didn't want to fight with Brother Rabbit, so finally he agreed, "Yes, I guess your runt pup did catch that deer," as he hopped off dejectedly into the woods calling for his fine hunting dog.

But once Brother Frog got far enough into the woods to be out of sight of Brother Rabbit his demeanor changed. He picked up a large stick and began beating it vigorously against a sweetgum tree.

BAM! BAM! BAM!

And with every lick Brother Frog gave the tree he hollered, "No Mister Man! No Mister Man! It wasn't my dog that caught your deer!"

BAM! BAM! BAM!

"No Mister Man! No Mister Man!"

BAM! BAM! BAM!

"It was Brother Rabbit's runt pup that caught your deer!"

BAM! BAM! BAM!

Hearing the racket, Brother Rabbit, who had started to skin out the deer, stood stock-still. He listened to the yelling and the beating as it came closer and closer. In a flash he grabbed up his runt pup and tucked it under his arm.

Then, at the top of his lungs, Brother Rabbit began yelling, "It sure wasn't my runt pup that caught that deer! How could a runt pup catch a deer?" Then he added, "It was Brother Frog's fine hunting dog that caught that deer for sure!" as he took off running for home.

When Brother Rabbit had disappeared into the trees, Brother Frog lay down his stick, came out of the woods, and finished skinning out the deer. Then he gathered up his meat, called to his fine hunting dog, and hopped slowly on home, smiling and swallowing all the way.

Finally, Miss Genevieve told me how Brother Rabbit, always trying to play the trickster, was once more out-tricked, this time by Brother Guinea Fowl . . .

One day Brother Rabbit and Brother Guinea were walking together in the woods when they came upon a cow grazing in a clearing. They could find no brand or mark on the cow so, clearly, this cow now belonged to them. After some discussion they agreed to butcher the cow and split the meat evenly. So they did.

When the meat was divided up equally into two piles Brother Rabbit remarked, "All that work made me so hungry! I can't wait for a meal of this good cow meat. Brother Guinea, why don't you fly up there in the sky and grab a piece of that orange fire. Bring it back here while I gather up some wood. We'll make a nice fire and cook a piece of this meat to eat right now."

Brother Guinea wasn't too sure about that plan, but at Brother Rabbit's urging he started flying toward the orange ball of fire in the sky. He flew and he flew but he never seemed to get any closer to it. Finally he was so worn out that he had to turn back.

When Brother Guinea at last returned to where he and Brother Rabbit had butchered the cow, all he saw was Brother Rabbit sitting by a pile of sticks at the edge of the clearing. The meat was all gone expect for the scrawny cow tail.

"Where's all our meat?" demanded Brother Guinea!

"I don't know," replied Brother Rabbit. "You were gone so long that I lay down to take a nap after I gathered this wood. When I woke up the meat was gone except for this scrawny tail here. Somebody must have stolen our meat!"

Brother Guinea studied this for a while, then grumbled, "Well, I am so tired and hungry that I have got to have something to eat. At least I can pick at this scrawny tail." And he did.

As Brother Guinea finished the last little scrap of meat on the scrawny tail he began to flop around, squawking and gasping.

"What's the matter?" asked Brother Rabbit in alarm!

"I'm poisoned! I'm poisoned!" shouted Brother Guinea.
With that, he flopped over on his back in the middle of the clearing . . . wings outstretched . . . dead.

"Oh no! Oh no!" cried Brother Rabbit, wringing his hands. "That meat was poisoned! What shall I do? I've got to get it back from my kinfolks! I don't want my whole family to die!"

Brother Rabbit raced around to all his many kinfolk, gathering up the meat that he had secretly carried off and distributed to them while Brother Guinea was gone. He brought it all back, piece by piece, and piled it up in the middle of the clearing.

As Brother Rabbit arrived with the last piece of meat, Brother Guinea jumped up, suddenly resurrected from the dead!

Brother Rabbit stared in astonishment. Brother Guinea shook his wing at Brother Rabbit declaring, "You thought you could fool me any time you wanted! You fooled me about the fire but you can't fool me all the time! Now we are going to share this meat evenly!"

And they did.

Crab Boy's Ghost

Cousin Corrie loved ghost stories and anything related to the supernatural, from ancient Egyptian tales of the mystical powers of cats to present-day theories of ESP. She often entertained teenage cousins with "table turning," an old-fashioned group activity designed to contact the spirit world. Like many in the Lowcountry, Cousin Corrie had grown up accepting the spirit world as just another aspect of reality, whether this spirit world was based on religious beliefs preached from the Sunday pulpit or on the folklore of haunts, hags, and plat-eyes that she learned from her Gullah family servants. The story of Crab Boy was one she heard as a child in her home at Woodlawn on the creek at Murrells Inlet. She especially liked telling it to children.

W hen I was a child we lived in a big wooden house right on the seashore at Murrells Inlet. Sometimes, early in the morning we would hear faint but urgent screams coming over and over from far down the creek toward Drunken Jack Island, behind what is now Huntington Beach. My mother, who didn't stand for any such nonsense, always said it was just a peacock calling from a distant farmyard. But the Gullah women who helped my mother in the kitchen told us children that it was the ghost of Crab Boy crying for help. They called such spirits of children who had died unnatural deaths "drolls."

Saltwater creeks and marshes between sandy barrier islands like Huntington Beach and the mainland seashore are full of sea life. This sea life becomes delicious seafood for those who know how to catch it. As children, my brothers and sisters and I caught fish, raked oysters, and dug for clams. My father and brothers caught shrimp in hand thrown nets. We easily attracted blue crabs with a fish head tied to a length of twine as they swam in on the rising tide. Once a crab was feeding, we pulled the fish head in slowly until the crab was close enough to "swoop" it up with a dip net. Sometimes we would see crabs just resting along the water's edge and could scoop them up without even needing fish heads.

Oysters, blue crabs, and clams all make delicious eating but the greatest delicacy of the marsh is the stone crab, with sweet juicy meat in its giant claw. Catching stone crabs requires a very different technique than catching blue crabs however. Stone crabs do not swim in and out with the tide. They live deep in burrows in the mud banks along the creeks. The burrows are only exposed at low tide. Catching a stone crab requires a highly skilled technique and a lot of courage. That giant claw that is so delicious to eat can crush a finger with little effort.

The best way to catch a stone crab is to wait for low tide, then walk along the edge of the creek looking for stone crab burrows. When you see one, which is just about as big around as your fist, you slowly slide your hand and arm way into it until you feel the crab with your fingers. Then you gently grab the crab "just the right way" and slip it out of the burrow and into your bucket. If the crab senses danger it will wedge itself in its hole with its legs and shell and attack with that giant claw.

Now this method of catching stone crabs has been carefully explained to me, don't you understand? I would never try it myself. Not after growing up hearing stories of Crab Boy!

No one ever seemed to know what Crab Boy's real name was. He wasn't from around these parts. He came down to stay with relatives that lived here at Murrells Inlet near the shore behind Drunken Jack Island on land that is now part of Brookgreen Gardens. Before Freedom, Crab Boy's uncles had been slaves here on the Waccamaw Neck on Brookgreen Plantation, or was it at The Oaks? Anyway, their job had been to provide all kinds of seafood for the planter's table. After Freedom, they remained at Murrells Inlet living off the bounty of its creeks and marshes.

Crab Boy's uncles and cousins caught all manner of seafood that they sold to the people living in cottages from Magnolia Beach all the way to the north end of Murrells Inlet at Sunnyside. Stone crab claws brought the most money but stone crabs took patience and skill to catch.

Crab Boy's relatives took him along as they gathered their harvest from the creeks. He learned to cast a shrimp net and to gather oysters carefully so as not to cut himself on their razor sharp shells. However his uncles warned him repeatedly, "Never go after stone crabs the way we do until you are much older."

Did he listen? Of course not!

One day when the tide was just past its low point Crab Boy was exploring the maze of creeks by himself when he saw a perfect stone crab hole. He had seen his uncles pull crabs out so easily that he was sure he could do it too.

The boy crouched down to the thick dark mud surrounding the hole and slowly reached in farther and farther until nearly his whole arm was extended into the burrow. Finally his fingers contacted the hard sharp creature. As he tried to slide his hand under the shell, the crab grabbed his finger with its crushing grip.

Crab Boy shrieked in pain! He tried to yank his arm out of the hole but it wouldn't budge! The crab had wedged itself solidly in the burrow and would not release its grip on the boy's finger.

Crab Boy screamed louder and louder for help. His uncles heard the cries and began searching for him but in the maze of creeks and marshes his calls seemed to come from every direction! His frantic relatives searched and searched until the rising tide stilled his voice. They found Crab Boy's lifeless body at the next low tide, his arm still trapped in the stone crab's burrow.

As a child I always wondered how they ever got his arm out so they could bury Crab Boy. Nobody ever answered that question for me. But whenever we children went out into the marsh they always reminded us to leave stone crabs alone. And whenever we heard the droll shrieking from down toward Drunken Jack Island they told us the story of Crab Boy.

Now even though these stories frightened us, they probably served a useful purpose: to keep us children from fooling around in the mud and putting our hands where they didn't belong. And they certainly worked for me! To this day I won't reach my hand into any hole in the creek bank.

The local people say Mrs. Chandler, here, is the only white woman in Murrells Inlet who can catch stone crabs. She can, too! I think it's because she didn't live here at the Inlet when she was little so she didn't hear the stories about Crab Boy until she was older. Those of us who did are just too scared to try!

Crab Boy's Ghost

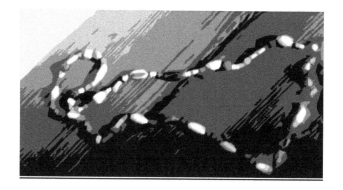

The Wachesaw Ghosts

On the top shelf inside the postcard display cases over by the front door of the Brookgreen Gardens Museum lay a string of small, dull-colored, blue, tan, and red beads carelessly strung on what looked like an old piece of frayed twine. The beads never looked like much to me. I paid them little attention until a visitor asked about them one morning. Then Miss Genevieve produced the most spine-tingling story in her repertoire—at least to my young ears. After that, I never entered or left the Museum without warily eyeing that strand of beads and wondering just what went on in the Museum after we had all gone home for the night.

"I won't die for a few teeth and arrowheads!" muttered James determinedly as he placed a bundle wrapped in a croaker sack uneasily on the ground. Glancing up at the archeologist supervising the dig, the haunted-looking laborer continued more loudly but in a voice filled with remorse, "Boss, I've come to confess."

The archeological dig where James worked had caused a lot of excitement around here that summer but had really come about by accident. My father bought Wachesaw Plantation, just up the Waccamaw Neck from Brookgreen Gardens, in the early part of this century. Like most plantations on the Waccamaw Neck, Wachesaw stretched in a narrow east-west band from Wachesaw Landing on the Waccamaw River to the seashore there at

Murrells Inlet and then on across the marsh to the ocean at Flagg's Landing, now called Garden City Beach.

Of course, by the time we moved here the days of vast rice fields and great plantation mansions were long gone. My family moved into the Hermitage, Dr. Allard Belin Flagg's old home on the edge of the creeks and marshes at Murrells Inlet. We raised chickens for our own use and grew vegetables and flowers in the gardens around the house but Papa made his living as a traveling salesman. Later, financial demands forced him to sell the main body of the plantation around Wachesaw Landing on the Waccamaw River, and the beach property at Flagg's Landing. He kept only the small portion of seashore at Murrells Inlet around the Hermitage where we continued to live.

A wealthy sportsman from New York named William Kimbel bought the main part of Wachesaw Plantation around Wachesaw Landing to use as a vacation retreat and a duck hunting preserve. Thousands of ducks rested and fed in the old rice fields every year during their spring and fall migrations. You would not believe how thick the sky was with them! My husband, Tom Chandler, went to work for Mr. Kimbel as caretaker and manager of the plantation.

Now, I don't know if Dr. Allard had ever built a real plantation mansion on Wachesaw. If he did, I never saw evidence of it. But Mr. Kimbel decided that he wanted a hunting lodge at Wachesaw Landing to use when he and his friends came South for the duck hunting. He asked my husband to supervise the construction.

Tom and Mr. Kimbel chose a lovely spot for the lodge on a bluff overlooking the Waccamaw River. But when workers began digging the foundation for the lodge, the first things they came across were long buried skeletons, many of them belonging to children. The arrangement of the skeletons and the beads and axes and

98

pottery jars buried with the bones indicated this land had been an Indian burial ground.

Tom immediately halted work on the lodge and contacted the Charleston Museum to see if they were interested in excavating the site. With only a little delay, they sent one scientist, and then several others, and the construction site soon became an archeological dig site. We were all thrilled, I was anyway, to become a part of a real archeological dig!

We had read all about the archeological treasures being discovered in Egypt: King Tut's tomb and everything. I was excited to have a real "dig" in our own back yard. Of course, we didn't expect to find gold statues and jewelry like Howard Carter and Lord Carnarvon had discovered in King Tut's tomb . . . but one never knows.

Tom had other duties in managing the plantation but I was at the dig site almost every day. I watched the excavations and talked with the scientists as they directed local workers in their careful trenching and sifting for artifacts. I often jumped down in there with them, uncovering the ancient bones and pottery. It was exciting!

The local workers, who were used to finding occasional arrowheads or broken pieces of pottery in the pinelands or along the beach, were not impressed with the finds at first. Their biggest concern appeared to be their uneasiness in digging up bones. Many would not work on the project because they believed that graves, whether white, black, or Indian, should never be disturbed.

As with any unusual occurrence, rumors began to spread among the local people. Warnings of dire happenings were whispered from person to person. Stories circulated about loud wailings from Wachesaw Bluff echoing through the night. None of us ever heard any wailing, and I'm not sure what local people would have gotten close enough to the diggings at night to hear such wailings, but the stories grew. Every sickness and stubbed toe was blamed on our disturbing the dead.

Then one of my daughters came down with diphtheria! In those times before antibiotics and modern treatments, diphtheria was a life threatening illness. I suffered through many fearful days and nights before she finally recovered. Thinking about it, it was kind of unusual. Normally with diphtheria there is an outbreak and the infection can be traced from person to person, often by contact or contaminated food, I believe. But this was just the one case, and everyone said it must have come from the graves of the Indian children who had probably died in an outbreak. Of course, by the time the stories got around we were having a sweeping epidemic of fatal disease caused by the curses of the dead in retribution for desecrating their graves.

Feelings are pretty high and beliefs are pretty strong around here about the sanctity of graves. Not so much anymore, but in past times, out in the small private graveyards back in the woods, you would see little objects left on graves, either on the headstones or on the graves themselves. They might include a cup or a bowl, a favorite knife or comb, or some small household object or tool that had belonged to the deceased. Sometimes these were used as containers to hold bunches of wild flowers but often the objects just sat on the graves. They were usually something meaningful to the deceased.

Some say these objects were placed on graves, like flowers, in honor and remembrance of the dead. Others say that favorite objects were left on graves so that restless spirits of the deceased would come looking for them there and not in their former homes where the living carried on their lives. Local people often told stories of uneasy spirits who repeatedly returned to their earthly homes until the correct favorite object was placed on the grave. In fact, one of those restless spirits seems to be looking for her ring in my family home (but you already know about Alice).

Whatever the reason for placing an object on the grave, these objects are usually left there undisturbed, sometimes for years. All know that dire consequences follow when any grave object is removed (but that's still another story, actually several other stories).

So it was only to be expected that when archeological excavations began, great distress arose among the local people that graves were being disturbed. Many would not help with the excavations. Those who did must have been less fearful of the supernatural world, or been in greater need of the excellent wages paid by the museum scientists.

The men who did work soon caught the enthusiasm and excitement the archeologists displayed at each new discovery. The scientists' excitement over a cache of small beads or a shell bracelet or a chipped stone ax quickly created awe among the workers for each seemingly plain object. There was much talk of how "valuable" each piece was. Of course, the scientists were referring to the value of knowledge about the past that each item imparted. No one realized workers had begun to believe that these items had great monetary value.

Now, I understand that on some archeological digs where artifacts of gold or precious jewels might be found, it is common practice to pay workers handsomely for each find so that they turn in valuable objects when they discover them and artifacts are not lost to the black market. None of the archeologists from Charleston ever considered that our workers might view these objects as worth concealing for monetary gain. They didn't realize the effects of their enthusiasm until that morning when James approached the scientist in charge. They only began to understand as they listened to James' unusual story.

~   ~   ~

Once James understood how valuable the artifacts were (he explained) it was hard to resist pocketing just a few. He thought happily about being able to sell them for much-needed cash or supplies. He knew he would have to take them to a big town to make any real money but figured his brother, who worked for the railroad in Florence, could help the next time he came home on a visit.

Soon James had quite a collection of relicts in his small cabin: arrowheads, hands full of beads, and several small axes. He had also collected a pocketful of loose teeth, which he kept in a coffee can on his mantel. James felt bad about taking objects but tried to look at it just as extra pay for a job no one else had the courage to take on. He also reasoned that money from the artifacts would be much more important to him than to Mr. Kimbel, who already had more money than anyone needed.

Still, James' conscience bothered him and he didn't sleep well at night even though he was tired from the excavation work. Tossing and turning one night, he gradually realized that way off in the distance he could hear the wailing voices that everybody talked about, or was it just wind in the pines? Each successive night he slept more poorly, between worrying about his stealing (because that was what he was having to admit he was doing) and listening for wailing or other strange noises outside in the night.

One night the noises were no longer outside. They came from inside the cabin, right there with James! He awoke to rattling sounds from the coffee can on his mantel and strange low murmurs from shadows passing in front of the window. As James lay stark still in his bed, the noises grew fainter and the sound of his pounding heart grew louder. He lay there like that until the sun came up, by which time he had convinced himself that he had just had a bad dream.

Still, it was even harder to get to sleep the next night and close to morning James again awakened with a start to the same rattling noises and moving shadows, only this time their voices were louder and their tone was angry. He could not make out any words but the shadows were clearly men and it looked like they were waving weapons at him! Fear clutched his heart. He could hardly breathe, much less move. The next thing James knew, he awoke to sun streaming in the window, relieved to be awake, alive, and away from his horrible nightmare.

The next night James once more lay down to sleep with great trepidation in spite of his increasing exhaustion. His anxiety was heightened by distant thunder that signaled a building storm. In spite of his fears, James quickly fell asleep. A clap of thunder soon woke him to a frightening spectacle however. Flashing lightning illuminated a group of angry Indian braves decked out in skins and feathers there in the room with him, shaking their spears and tomahawks at him! Frozen with fear, James could hear chanting and shouting as well as rattling and pounding, even over the thunderclaps. The Indian braves stomped and gestured directly at him ever more wildly! Suddenly a gigantic flash of lightning and a thunderous crash shook the cabin! In that flash the braves in their regalia vanished but the coffee can hurtled off the mantel, scattering teeth all across the floor.

James sat bolt upright in bed, terrified. Thunder and lightning continued but the braves never returned. James lit a lamp and sat up the remainder of the night, wide-awake, but he was not visited again.

At dawn, James bundled up the artifacts, getting down on his hands and knees to search out every last tooth from under his sparse furniture. He took the bundle straight to the dig and presented it, along with his confession, to the scientist in charge that morning.

James begged to be allowed to continue working on the dig because he was in great need of money. The scientist accepted his confession, along with the return of the stolen items, and agreed to let James keep working. Here was one worker who certainly wasn't going to carry off any more artifacts!

Later that morning the scientist called a meeting of all the workers. He carefully explained that, while the artifacts were priceless for the information they gave us, they had little real monetary value. He did offer rewards for any special pieces the men found that they thought they might be able to sell elsewhere, just to encourage the workers' honesty.

~   ~   ~

When their excavations were completed, the Charleston scientists, with Mr. Kimbel's permission, were kind enough to encourage me to select a souvenir of the dig in appreciation for my assistance. I chose these beads for several reasons. They were women's ornaments and I felt a kinship with the women who, like me, must have worried about their stricken children. The beads had obviously been important to them; they had left them with their most precious objects, their children.

I also chose the beads because they were lovely. Their pale, soft colors must have ornamented special costumes in happier days.

Finally, I chose these beads because I knew they had a story that went back even further than the Indian people who buried them at Wachesaw. I knew this because these beads are made of glass.

While Indians made beads of shell and stone, they did not possess the craft of glass making. So Europeans, not Indians, made these beads. They most likely originated in the glass furnaces of the tiny island of Murano in the Venetian lagoon, long before Italy even existed as a country, perhaps before the mothers who buried these beads with their children were born. The breath that formed the fine hollow tubes that would be cut and polished into these individual beads also formed words in the dialect of Marco Polo.

Glass blowers of Murano created these beads for trade with native peoples and sold them over the centuries to explorers and traders heading for the gradually expanding New World. Spanish settlers with Lucas Vasquez de Ayllon near here at Chicora, who were the first Europeans to settle in South Carolina, may have carried these beads across the Atlantic in their small sailing ships. Or Miss Dusenbury's ancestors, early Carolina fur traders of English descent, may have brought them up from Charleston by dugout canoe to exchange with the Waccamaws or Winyahs for deer hides, which they sent back to England by way of Charleston. Or these beads may have made their way overland to us along native trade routes through the western mountains, acquired from French traders coming up the Mississippi or down from Hudson's Bay. They may even have arrived in South Carolina along coastal trade routes, passed on by natives who originally received them from Dutch settlers in exchange for land on Manhattan.

Yes, these beads have a long history that involves gondolas and sailing ships and dugout canoes, or perhaps pack mules, as well as all varieties of adventurers and traders, before they ever reached graves here at Wachesaw. And who knows where their path will lead over the next centuries. I am happy to be a small part of their history, like those Indian mothers who treasured them for a brief period, then left them with their precious lost children.

~   ~   ~

I have never felt any sad or threatening emanations from these beads. I truly believe the previous owners were kindred spirits who would have wanted these beads to continue to bring joy and comfort to their owners. But I will tell you a little more of their story that does raise some tiny doubts in my mind.

Brookgreen Gardens is open to visitors during the day but closes at five o'clock every evening. The front gates are locked, as are the doors to the few buildings such as the Old Kitchen and this building, the Museum. We have rarely had any problems after hours but a night watchman patrols the grounds throughout the night just to make sure. The night watchman follows set rounds on a set schedule. He carries a time clock with him and must punch it at set intervals with keys attached to various boxes around the Gardens to show that he is actually on the job.

One of the time clock key boxes is located on the back wall of the second of the two small-sculpture galleries attached here to the Museum. Each gallery is formed by a rectangle of twelve-foot-high gray-brick walls, mostly covered with ivy. Small sculptures are displayed inside along the brick walls with the center of each gallery open to the sky. Several times each night the night watchman must unlock the front door of the Museum, pass through this part of the building containing the postcard display cabinets that also hold the Wachesaw beads, go through the first small-sculpture gallery, then enter the second small-sculpture gallery. There, on a chain in a little metal box attached to the brick wall at the very back of this second gallery, he finds the time clock key for this location and uses it to punch his time clock.

Now our night watchman is not a fanciful man, but often at night when he is on the front porch preparing to enter the Museum, or when he is in the Museum, or in the open-air galleries heading for the time clock key box, noises come to him, rising and falling like distant voices wailing.

Are ancient spirits who once owned the Wachesaw beads still mourning their long lost relatives? Are ghosts of long dead Indians trying to reclaim property taken from their graves? I cannot answer that for you. You must decide for yourself.

I will tell you one possible explanation for the wailing. If you look closely at the brick walls here at Brookgreen Gardens, including the walls of the small-sculpture galleries, you will see that they are not solid. Spaces between the bricks form a lattice pattern. This saves on the number of bricks needed to make the walls and also creates an attractive openwork design.

Some people say that as night winds blow around these walls, the holes between the bricks cause peculiar whistling or wailing noises. That could certainly be true. Or perhaps Indian spirits still want to make their presence known around my Wachesaw beads.

The Great Sandy Island Expedition

Like many young people in the 1950s and '60s, I was caught up in the revival of popular interest in folk music. My enjoyment of Kingston Trio records led to a curiosity about more authentic roots of our American folk tunes. I was so thrilled to receive a copy of the fascinating anthology, The Folk Songs of North America, *by Alan Lomax, that I carried it everywhere with me, including to Murrells Inlet.*

"You should show Miss Genevieve this book," Cousin Corrie suggested after I shared some entries with her. "I think she knows the man who wrote it."

I smiled indulgently at Cousin Corrie. In my young mind I couldn't conceive of our plain old Miss Genevieve as ever knowing anyone important enough to write such an impressive book. Reluctantly, to humor Cousin Corrie, I brought the book with me the next time I visited Brookgreen Gardens.

I was right, of course. Miss Genevieve didn't know Alan Lomax at all. The man she knew was his father, John Lomax, the person responsible for the most important collection of American folk song and folklore recordings in the world today, the same John Lomax whose recordings and writings had fueled the entire folk song revival that so captured my interest!

I first got to know Mr. Lomax when I went to work for the WPA in the 1930s (Miss Genevieve explained). Our country went through a terrible Depression at that time. The prices of cotton and tobacco fell drastically here in South Carolina. People couldn't make a living farming and many lost their farms and their homes. The textile manufacturing plants closed too. So many people were out of work! And no welfare or Social Security to support them.

Mr. Roosevelt in Washington knew that something had to be done so he started all sorts of government programs as a part of his New Deal to put people back to work. One of the most important programs was the Works Projects Administration. A division of the WPA hired workers to build roads and parks and government buildings all over the country and then hired artists and craftsmen to decorate them, leaving us a marvelous legacy.

The part of the WPA that affected me was the Federal Writers' Project. My husband had died, leaving me with five young children to support. I was fortunate enough to get a position with the Federal Writers' Project because I had done some writing off and on over the years, mainly short pieces about our local culture for New York magazines.

Working for the WPA Writers' Project was one of the most interesting jobs I have ever held. Our best-known accomplishment was publishing the WPA Guide to South Carolina. Each state in the Union wrote a travel guide for that state that also included sections on its history, geography, economy, and culture. You can still find copies of these in many public libraries and they still make wonderful guides for exploring the states.

To me, an even more interesting WPA project involved writing up interviews with former slaves and collecting folktales and folk songs from them and from other local people. I got to know Mr. Lomax because he was Folklore Editor for the Federal Writers' Project. For years he had been collecting folk songs and stories from all over the South. He wanted to record traditional songs of local people before radio and phonograph records changed everything. When he read over the stories and songs I had collected, he recognized how alive the unique Gullah culture remained in our area.

Mr. Lomax and I corresponded regularly and he began including Murrells Inlet on his recording tours of the South. Fortunately, I was able to introduce him to a number of local people and persuade them to sing and tell stories into his recording equipment.

Mr. Lomax came to visit us here at Murrells Inlet several times over the years. He always brought his recording equipment and he usually brought his wife, who helped with the recording and kept notes on people and places he visited. She also tried to smooth over her husband's lack of social graces. Mr. Lomax was from Texas, don't you know. He talked like a cowboy and he acted like one too: kind of rough and not too civilized but very kind and friendly. The local people always remembered Mr. Lomax as that Texas cowboy who wanted to hear old time singing. Lots of people around here sang for him, both white people and black people.

Mr. Lomax had some fancy recording equipment owned by the Library of Congress, the government agency that sent him out to collect songs. When he could, he hooked up his recording equipment to electrical power but when that wasn't available he had big heavy batteries, sort of like our car batteries today, that could run the recording equipment for more than an hour. He carried it all, several hundred pounds worth, in the trunk of his Ford sedan.

The recording machine itself looked a lot like a big bulky phonograph. There was a turntable and an arm with a needle attached to it. When he put a blank record on the turntable, set the needle on the disk, and turned the machine on, the record went around and around and the needle cut grooves in it recording the sound that came from the microphone. The microphone was a big box attached by wires to the recording machine. The wires were quite long so the singer and microphone did not have to be right by the recording machine.

Not all houses in this area had electricity at that time but the house where we lived with my father, the Hermitage, did, so Mr. Lomax often set up his recording equipment there. He would put the recording machine in the sitting room but would stretch the microphone wires out onto the porch where the singers preferred to perform because it was cooler there. He would operate the recording machine himself inside the house while Mrs. Lomax, outside, would announce the song or singer on the record and make sure they stood close enough to the microphone.

The records were 78s of course back then so there were only a few minutes of music on each side of the disk. Mr. and Mrs. Lomax had to carry boxes and boxes of records with them in the car in addition to the recording equipment and batteries, and their suitcases too of course. They were usually pretty heavily loaded when they pulled in to see me.

Mr. and Mrs. Lomax always spent time touring Brookgreen Gardens whenever they visited Murrells Inlet. Walking among the ancient live oak trees hung with Spanish moss was a special delight for them whether they came in summer when flowers were blooming or in winter when the Gardens were subdued in greens and grays.

When Mr. Lomax visited us here, it was always as part of a grand tour of several Southern states. The tours usually lasted a month or two as he visited Virginia, North Carolina, South Carolina, Georgia, Florida, Mississippi,

Alabama, Texas, and maybe others. He usually stayed with us several days in Murrells Inlet. This was one of his main locations for Gullah, the creole language and culture developed by coastal Carolina slaves. Back then, lots of former slaves and their families still spoke Gullah, or at least understood it.

Those must have been adventurous expeditions for Mr. Lomax and his wife. They usually traveled along main highways and most of those, like the King's Highway, were paved by then but it was still a long way between towns if car trouble developed.

And it seemed like one thing or another was always interfering with his recordings—at least here in Murrells Inlet. One time, all the singers I had arranged for him to record got into some kind of family dispute and all refused to come sing for Mr. Lomax. I was able to find some other people to sing at the last minute but it was a confusion and he missed a lot of the songs I wanted him to record.

Another time, something was wrong with his recording needle and it had spoiled some disks. By the time he got to Murrells Inlet, he was down to his last few records and had to limit the number of songs he recorded.

One summer, there was a terrible polio epidemic in our area. Summers used to be dreadful that way. Thank goodness we don't have those anymore! That summer I had arranged to gather a group of local children together for Mr. Lomax to record play-party songs and rhymes, but then all gatherings of children were banned to try to control the spread of the disease. Once again, I had to find substitutes for the planned recordings.

Another visit presented a series of equally daunting obstacles at each turn but we managed to overcome them all and accomplish the most wonderful recordings of any of his visits, in my mind. We made some of these recordings

in Murrells Inlet but we made some of these special re-
cordings in a very special location. Today Brookgreen
Gardens includes part of this unique place called Sandy
Island.

Now Sandy Island isn't really on the Waccamaw
Neck but it borders it. Here in Georgetown County, the
Waccamaw River runs pretty much straight from north to
south, parallel to the seacoast and only three or four miles
inland, until it empties into Winyah Bay off Georgetown.
The Waccamaw Neck is that strip of land between the
Waccamaw River and the ocean.

Well, about a mile farther inland from of the Waccamaw River, another river also runs north to south
parallel to the Waccamaw River and also flows into Winyah
Bay near Georgetown. This is the Pee Dee River. Along the
whole length of where these two rivers run parallel to each
other, little cross-streams connect the two rivers. The Waccamaw is a little lower than the Pee Dee so these little
cross-streams drain water from the Pee Dee into the Waccamaw River all the way along. These two rivers are about
the same size when they enter Georgetown County from
the north but by the time they get to Winyah Bay, the Waccamaw is huge, more than a mile across, while the Pee Dee
is pretty small, even though the Black River joins it just before it gets to the bay.

The cross-streams divide the swampy sandy land
between the two rivers into islands, the biggest of which is
Sandy Island. A good-sized cross-stream called Bull Creek
(you remember, part of the Confederate trade routes) borders Sandy Island on its north end and a medium-sized
cross-stream called Thoroughfare Creek borders it on its
south end. Of course, the Waccamaw borders it on the east
side and the Pee Dee on the west side.

Sandy Island was always prime rice growing country. In fact, nine different rice plantations developed there,

but most of the planters who owned them lived on the Waccamaw Neck or in Georgetown or Charleston. Sandy Island was isolated even in those days. Most slaves on Sandy Island were descendants of Africans who had been brought over in the 1700s. Very few slaves left Sandy Island and very few came from the outside in later years. The Gullah language and culture developed among slaves there until Gullah came to be the primary language spoken on Sandy Island, as on many plantations in the Lowcountry.

The Gullah Language

Nobody can tell you for sure how the Gullah language developed but people who have studied it do have some idea about its history and this is how they explain it.

Slaves brought to South Carolina came from different parts of West Africa. Each African area and tribal group had its own language and customs. When slaves arrived on Lowcountry plantations, communication was a big challenge. Slaves and planters spoke different languages and often fellow slaves even spoke different languages yet all had to understand each other well enough to live and work together.

A pidgin language developed that contained words and grammatical structures from English and from various African languages. Planters and overseers kept speaking English and slaves kept speaking their own various languages but each also learned to speak the pidgin language, called Gullah, to communicate with each other. People who study languages tell me that at this stage Gullah was a pidgin language because no one spoke it as his native language but those speaking different languages used it to communicate with each other. Some people think the name Gullah came from the word Angola, which was the homeland of many of the slaves.

As new generations of slaves were born in the Low-country, these children grew up speaking Gullah as their native language. Gullah became a creole language, which is one whose words and grammar are a combination of different languages but one which is now the native language of a group of people, in this case, the descendants of the slaves brought from Africa.

Planters and other whites continued to speak English, of course, but also spoke Gullah to communicate with their workers. Planters and their families often learned Gullah as children from nurses and other household servants who helped raise them.

On Sandy Island before the War Between the States, Dr. Edward Heriot's Mont Arena Plantation, where the main river landing was located, became the center of activity. Dr. Heriot's friend, Captain Thomas Petigru, planted nearby Pipedown Plantation. Unlike most other men who owned plantations on Sandy Island, Dr. Heriot and Captain Petigru and their families actually lived there on their plantations.

Shortly before the War Captain Petigru died. His widow moved away and no longer wanted to operate Pipedown Plantation. She began looking for a buyer for the plantation and contacted several large landowners in the area but none was interested.

Pipedown slaves grew worried. They feared the Petigru family would abandon the plantation and send their slaves off to auction, separating them from their home and from each other.

So Sandy Island slaves took matters into their own hands in one of the few ways permitted to them by the laws of that time. In quite an unusual step, and one that demonstrated a unique level of independence and initiative, Pipedown slaves met together to select a new master for themselves! They discussed what they knew about each planter under consideration: the clothing, food, medical services, and religious opportunities he provided for his slaves; the type of overseers he hired; the disciplinary measures he used; and his history of buying and selling off slaves.

After much discussion, Pipedown slaves settled on Governor Robert Francis Withers Allston, who already owned lands on the Pee Dee River, to become their new master. Governor Allston was the son of Benjamin Allston who had inherited Brookgreen Plantation from his father, Gentleman Billy Allston, the Revolutionary War guerrilla fighter who married Rachel Moore, later Rachel Moore Allston Flagg. (Remember, I told you all these stories, like all these families, are connected. Ask me about Governor Allston's three given names sometime. They have an interesting story behind them that also forms a part of the history of Brookgreen.) Anyway, the Pipedown slaves all agreed that Governor Allston would make the best new master.

The next step was to convince Governor Allston! The Widow Petigru had already offered Pipedown and its slaves to Governor Allston but he had turned her down saying that he already owned more than enough land and slaves. (As it turned out, he was right, but that's another story.) So Sandy Islanders had quite a task ahead of them.

The community met again and selected Phillip Washington, the Pipedown Driver, to carry their request to Governor Allston. They chose Phillip Washington because he was intelligent and better educated than many of the other slaves. He was also well spoken and a leader respected by both his fellow slaves and by white planters.

The trip to Governor Allston was arranged. There Phillip Washington pleaded the case of the Pipedown slaves so eloquently that Governor Allston changed his mind, agreed to purchase Pipedown, and soon did so! The slaves of Pipedown had accomplished their goal. They had kept their community together and acquired themselves a new master of their own choosing.

~ ~ ~

The War caused disruptions on Sandy Island, as elsewhere, but very few slaves, or later, former slaves, left their homes there. For decades after Freedom Sandy Islanders maintained an isolated and independent community. They raised their own food and sold or traded rice for other necessities. The people of Sandy Island also preserved their Gullah culture and language like almost no other community. They kept their own customs and beliefs as well as their Gullah language long into the Twentieth Century.

Phillip Washington, Community Organizer

Phillip Washington was one of the few freed slaves who left Sandy Island after the War. Although he was reluctant to leave his family and the home he loved, he was eager to explore new opportunities open to him as a free man. He moved to Georgetown where Federal occupation in the years following the War allowed former slaves possibilities for advancement in business and politics.

Phillip Washington became quite successful in business and even purchased a home on Front Street in the wealthiest section of Georgetown.

Racial tensions ran high however, and when occupying Federal forces finally left in 1877, whites regained their former power. They moved rapidly to undo opportunities former slaves had enjoyed during the previous ten years.

The native Sandy Islander quickly recognized the changing political and economic realities. He realized that he and others like him could no longer prosper in white society but he soon hit upon an alternative plan. He determined to found an independent self-sufficient community of former slaves back on his beloved Sandy Island.

Phillip Washington sold his house in Georgetown and moved back home to Sandy Island where he began establishing his community. First of all, he purchased a few acres of Mont Arena land and organized residents there to build a church, which soon became the spiritual and political center of the community. It remains so today. Next, he rented neighboring abandoned rice fields from struggling absentee planters and hired out-of-work former slaves to raise a rice crop. Fortunately the harvest was successful.

Phillip Washington used profits from that first rice crop and the rest of the proceeds from the sale of his house in Georgetown to purchase all of Mont Arena Plantation. With this as its base, his community of organized and resourceful former slaves on Sandy Island continued to thrive and prosper growing rice, even after Phillip Washington died around the turn of the century.

Early in the Twentieth Century, wealthy Yankees began buying up former rice plantations for hunting preserves, including other plantations on Sandy Island. After some negotiations, the Northern owners agreed to let Sandy Islanders raise rice on their newly acquired island preserves without paying rent. It was good for the duck hunting.

Sandy Island remains isolated to this day. There are still alligators there and strange plants like the insect-eating Venus Flytrap. Rare little Red-cockaded Woodpeckers still nest in hollows of ancient long leaf pines. Some even say that huge red-headed Ivory-billed Woodpeckers still live there although they are extinct most places. No white people have lived on Sandy Island, I imagine, since the last Heriot family members left shortly after the War.

Prince Washington, grandson of Phillip Washington, has become a community leader and now, in the middle of the Twentieth Century, is encouraging some modernization. School children have started riding a ferry across the river to come to school here on the mainland. Many of the adults have started commuting off the island to day jobs at Brookgreen Gardens or Pawley's Island or even at Myrtle Beach, especially as the tourist industry has grown, but they still don't have electricity or telephones on the island. It remains a unique place.

Over the many years that I have been visiting Sandy Island I have gotten to know some of the islanders. One of the most interesting was Aunt Hagar Brown who lived here on the Waccamaw Neck but had close ties to Sandy Island. Aunt Hagar became one of my best and most enthusiastic informants when I was recording former slave narratives for the Federal Writers' Project in the 1930s.

When I told Mr. Lomax about Aunt Hagar and other Sandy Islanders, he was as excited as I was about making recordings of them telling their stories and singing their songs. Mr. Lomax and I corresponded several times about making sure Aunt Hagar and her people were available when he came to Murrells Inlet on his next recording trip. I assured him that I would have them ready to record.

My first obstacle, not entirely unexpected, was to get Aunt Hagar and the others to agree to meet and talk to Mr. Lomax. They talked readily to me about their life and their community but they weren't too sure they would have anything to say to this stranger. Outsiders, especially white men, and most especially white men from the government, rarely meant good news for Sandy Islanders.

Another obstacle to overcome with the Sandy Islanders was the idea of having their music and stories recorded. Most had heard music played from phonographs but some regarded these phonographs and phonograph records as instruments of the Devil. The whole idea of talking or singing into a record-making machine sounded suspicious to more than one.

After a good bit of talk on my part they finally agreed to meet Mr. Lomax but would make no promises from there on. I imagined that he would quickly make them feel comfortable and that everything would work out just fine. So I hadn't given the situation much more thought until a few days before Mr. Lomax was scheduled to arrive. Then I suddenly realized that I hadn't really thought through the logistics of getting Aunt Hagar, the Sandy Islanders, Mr. Lomax, and his equipment all together in the same place to make his recordings.

When I did start to consider this, my first thought was to have Aunt Hagar's people come over to the Hermitage for the day where we had electricity and could make our recordings with no trouble. That seemed like an easy and simple plan but Aunt Hagar soon put a stop to that notion. As much as she would like to please me and Mr. Lomax from Washington, her people had their own busy lives to tend to on Sandy Island and weren't about to pick up and leave them for anyone, especially under these strange circumstances!

What to do about this obstacle? The answer again seemed simple. We would just go over to Sandy Island to do the recording! After all, Mr. Lomax had batteries just so that he could record in places like that with no electricity.

Getting to Sandy Island was always easier said than done however. No roads ever connected Sandy Island to anyplace, and they still don't. The only way to get to Sandy Island is by boat.

Visiting Sandy Island usually took some hard rowing, even going and coming with the tide, whether from Wachesaw Landing or from the landing at Brookgreen. It had always been easy enough to find someone to take me though, but what was easy for me alone was not so easy when we needed to carry several people and several hundred pounds of recording equipment and batteries over the water. This was becoming quite an expedition!

Rowboats were easy to find but none of them was big enough and sturdy enough for our job. If Mr. Lomax had come during duck hunting season there would have been no difficulty at all. Yankee sportsmen up and down the river, like Mr. Kimbel at Wachesaw Plantation, had big comfortable cabin cruisers to take them out to hunting locations along the river. I'm sure they would have given us a ride. But it was summer and the boats were all stored away and most of the sportsmen had gone back up North. None of the workboats at Brookgreen Gardens was available either. Of course, there were several big powerful boats at docks in the salt-water creeks at Murrells Inlet but no easy way to get them around into the river.

I worried and fretted day and night over this obstacle. Mr. Lomax was already on his way to Murrells Inlet. Would I have to disappoint him? Finally, through a friend of Mr. Kimbel we were able to find some people down in Georgetown who thought it would make a lovely outing to bring their cabin cruiser upriver to Wachesaw Landing, spend a few nights at Murrells Inlet with friends, and transport us, our party, and our equipment over to Sandy Island for the day. What a relief! I could keep my promise to Mr. Lomax to record the Sandy Islanders!

By this point I was just waiting for the next obstacle to pop up. Yet everything went smoothly once Mr. Lomax arrived. I'm not sure Mr. Lomax had realized we would need to transport everything to Sandy Island by boat. And I know he was surprised when an oxcart met us at Mont Arena Landing to carry the recording machine, the records, the batteries, and our whole party up through the deeply rutted sand to Mont Arena Church where we set up the equipment. But he acted like it was the most natural thing in the world, traveling like this to get his recordings.

And the sessions with Aunt Hagar and the Sandy Islanders went beautifully. Mr. Lomax's friendly and informal ways were always quick to put people at ease. Once Aunt Hagar started talking, she went on and on. Others readily joined in, giving him much more than he had disks to record. He was able to record Aunt Hagar's stories about The Flagg Flood, some of her old-time songs from childhood, and answers to his inquiries about Sandy Island customs. His question about why door and window frames were painted blue ("To keep the evil spirits away!") even got her started on stories about haunts and hags and other supernatural creatures. Others added different songs and stories.

It was an extremely successful recording session and a perfectly delightful day for all of us. I don't think Mr.

Lomax ever knew how much worry and effort I had put into making it happen. He just believed I could produce whatever he needed with a snap of my fingers, which was a good feeling for me.

So somewhere, stored away in the Library of Congress with all the books ever printed in the United States, are the songs and stories of Aunt Hagar and her Sandy Island community, saved forever, just like we heard them that day on our Great Sandy Island Expedition. Maybe someday you will hear them too.

About the Author

Charles Town blacksmith William Green purchased his first land near that new Carolina settlement in 1695. His descendents have continued to live and thrive in the Carolina Lowcountry for more than three hundred years.

Lynn Michelsohn, one of William Green's ninth-generation granddaughters, was born not too far away in Durham, North Carolina. She grew up steeped in Lowcountry stories, as well as in the black mud of its tidal marshes. Her heart remains among the moss-draped live oaks lining the saltwater creeks of South Carolina's Waccamaw Neck. Now, she and her husband have two sons who love the Lowcountry almost as much as she does.

In *Tales from Brookgreen* this native Carolinian retells stories she heard from two early hostesses at Brookgreen Gardens: Mrs. Genevieve Wilcox Chandler and the author's cousin, Miss Corrie Dusenbury. Through these stories she conveys her sense of romance, history, and mystery hidden just beneath the serenely beautiful surface of Brookgreen Gardens, one of South Carolina's most popular tourist attractions.

The

author

as she

was . . .

and

remains

always

. . . in her heart

CPSIA information can be obtained
at www.ICGtesting.com
Printed in the USA
BVHW03s1228071018

529184BV00005B/312/P